Protecting young children

a guide to recognising and responding to child abuse

Helen Edwards

edited by Pat Gordon Smith

the national
**early years
network**

NSPCC
Cruelty to children

D0244015

The National Early Years Network
77 Holloway Road
London N7 8JZ
tel 020 7607 9573
email info@neyn.org.uk

© The National Early Years Network and NSPCC 2002

National Early Years Network registered charity no. 801041
NSPCC registered charity no. 216401

ISBN 1 870985 61 3

Designed by Susan Clarke for Expression, IP23 8HH

Cover photograph by Sarah-Vivien Prescott

The publication of this book was supported by printing and
binding that was generously carried out by HSBC.

Contents

Notes on this publication

Definitions

- The word 'parent' refers to the adult with legal responsibility for a child who will, in most cases, be the child's parent, but may be another family member, foster carer or other carer.
- A 'key person' is the early years practitioner who has the chief responsibility for a child in full day care or sessional care.
- A 'key worker' is the social worker who coordinates the help given to a family involved in a child protection investigation.

Using references

References to publications are shown in rounded brackets as the author followed by the date of publication, *eg* (Smith 1996). The relevant book or article can be found in the 'References' section by searching for the author's name and then for the correct date reference.

The square brackets contain references to sections within *Protecting young children*.

Case studies and exercises

Sections or chapters marked with this icon are case studies that are designed to help you see how the information in this book relates to situations which you might encounter.

The book contains opportunities for group training or individual reflection. They are marked by this icon.

UK jurisdictions

As in all matters of policy since devolution, the information on aspects of law and policy-related issues in this book are specific to England only. However, all guidance on good practice is applicable throughout the UK. Details of the child protection legal framework in the other UK countries are available on the following numbers:

- **Northern Ireland:** NSPCC, Belfast 028 9035 1135
- **Scotland:** Children 1st, Edinburgh 0131 337 8539
- **Wales:** NSPCC, Cardiff 029 2026 7000.

Acknowledgements

We would like to thank Trevor Spratt of Queen's University, Belfast, for his critical reading of the manuscript. The text was also read closely by Eva Lloyd, Chief Executive of the National Early Years Network and, at the NSPCC, by Christopher Cloke, head of child protection awareness, David Coulter, policy adviser in education and employment, and parenting adviser Eileen Hayes. The project was managed by Ro Gordon, head of consultancy at the NSPCC.

We are also grateful to Julie Jennings of the Royal National Institute for the Blind for her invaluable material on the abuse of children with disabilities (Chapter 5) and Jennie Lindon (author of Lindon 1998) for the practical example about Sam and Kimberley (pp. 8 and 12).

Foreword

Safeguarding and protecting young children is an essential part of any early years practitioner's role. With it comes the need to be aware of the relevant, current legislation and government guidance, and of good practice in this area. Given the particular vulnerability of young children and the welcome expansion in early years provision, it is likely that early years practitioners will need to deal with child protection concerns at some point in their career.

Legislation that is now being drawn up will place a clear responsibility for child protection on teachers, so early years practitioners will want and need to take their equivalent obligations very seriously indeed. NSPCC and the National Early Years Network have therefore collaborated on producing key information and practical advice aimed at helping them to do so.

One message that comes through loud and clear from the research underpinning this book is that early years practitioners can play a vital part in supporting families who find it difficult to meet their young children's needs, and so help prevent them becoming involved in the child protection system.

We are delighted to be publishing this timely book together. It will serve as a valuable resource for the initial child protection training for newly recruited early years practitioners required under the Care Standards Act 2000, and for teachers in nursery, infant and primary schools.

Eva Lloyd
Chief Executive, The National Early Years Network

Mary Marsh
Chief Executive, NSPCC

August 2002

Introduction

As a manager, practitioner, volunteer or helper in a child care setting, you aim to know the children in your care well, to know when they are happy and what they like or dislike. You know who looks after them at home, and parents will turn to you for advice and guidance. The children know you as someone they can trust, someone who looks after them and makes sure they are OK. This places you in a strong position to be vigilant about keeping them safe from harm.

This is very important because babies and very young children are more at risk of abuse than their older peers – they are smaller and less able to express their feelings or explain their experiences.

Given the particular vulnerability of young children, it is likely that you will deal with child protection concerns at some point in your career. Some children may already be on the child protection register when they arrive at your setting; a handful may become the subject of a child abuse inquiry. You or a colleague may even be accused of abuse.

Legislation and government guidance clearly set out the responsibilities and expectations of day care and early education services in safeguarding and protecting children, saying that 'all staff should be alert to the signs of abuse and neglect, and know to whom they should report concerns or suspicions' (Department of Health *et al.* 1999, para. 3.14).

Practitioners and organisations do not always understand their role in the protection of young children. Perhaps they don't know what to do, fear the parents or worry about what might happen to the child. They may not believe that abuse happens. But child abuse does happen, and intervention can both stop and prevent it. In fact, the National Commission of Inquiry into the Prevention of Child Abuse (1996) concluded that most cases of child abuse could be prevented so long as there was the will to do so.

People who work in the field of child protection know that thinking about how to respond to child abuse can cause great anxiety. Nobody expects you to become an expert in child protection and in identifying what is abuse; there are professionals in social services, the police, health, education and the NSPCC whose role it is to determine whether a child is at risk of or experiencing significant harm, and whether she is in need of protection.

But there is a lot you can do. Research has highlighted the important role played by early years practitioners in supporting children and families who have been referred to social services because of child protection or other concerns (Aldgate & Statham 2001).

The vast majority of children living in the UK lead happy, safe and protected lives in a caring environment. But there are some who do not, and we all have a duty to protect these children. Many people feel worried or scared when dealing with child protection, but it is vital to address the issues with confidence. This book aims to help early years providers, managers and practitioners gain that confidence and use it well by offering clear guidance through some of the legal, practical and emotional complexities connected with child protection and abuse. It aims to help practitioners identify young children who are being abused and to show what can be done to support them. It will also help practitioners comply with the child protection requirements in Standard 13 of the National Standards for Under Eights Day Care and Childminding (Department for Education and Employment 2001), and offers practical advice about how to help prevent children being abused in the first place.

Supporting families

The approach to child protection has changed over the past ten years. Research into child protection revealed that there was too great a focus on the investigation of suspected abuse and not enough on support services for children and families who find it difficult to meet their children's needs (Department of Health 1995).

Since 1997 the government has introduced a number of initiatives which are aimed at helping families cope. Early Years Development and Childcare Partnerships and Early Excellence Centres were set up to ensure an integrated early education and child care infrastructure. The introduction of financial support such as the child care tax credit aims to help parents back to work by helping them pay for child care. Other initiatives, including Sure Start, New Deal for Communities and the Healthy Living Centres, all add to the policy framework for supporting families. Government also funds a number of local parenting education projects and support programmes, and established the National Family and Parenting Institute – an independent charity which brings together organisations, knowledge and know-how to ensure that parents are supported in bringing up their children and in finding the help and information they need.

The National Early Years Network and the NSPCC believe that child protection forms part of the general need to promote a safe and happy life for all children. 'Child protection' protects children from abuse while 'safeguarding children' promotes the prevention of abuse and encourages children's welfare.

1 What is child abuse?

Child abuse is physical injury, emotional abuse, neglect or sexual abuse that is inflicted, or not prevented, and which causes 'significant harm' to or death of a child. Child abuse can be inflicted, or not prevented, by the person having care of the child, a person known to the child but not the carer, or by someone not known to the child. [There is an explanation of the term 'significant harm' under 'Section 47', p. 62.]

Categories of abuse

It is generally accepted that there are four main forms of abuse: physical abuse, emotional abuse, neglect and sexual abuse.

The following definitions are adapted from *Working together to safeguard children* (Department of Health *et al.* 1999).

1 Physical abuse

Physical abuse may involve hitting, shaking, throwing, poisoning, burning, scalding, drowning, suffocating or otherwise causing physical harm to a child. Physical harm may also be caused when parents or carers feign the symptoms of, or deliberately causes ill-health to, a child they are looking after. This situation is commonly described using terms such as 'fabricated or induced illness in children' or Munchausen Syndrome by Proxy (Wilson 2001).

Think it over

Different people have their own views of what constitutes child abuse. People draw upon what they have heard, what they have experienced, what they believe and what they value.

Take five minutes to consider these five scenarios and think about whether they might present child protection concerns. If possible, discuss your views with colleagues.

► Jill and Rachel are three-year-old twins. They have a sister, Suzy (10), and a brother, Andrew (11). Both parents work at the local bakers and have to juggle their shifts. Sometimes, maybe once a week, the shifts mean that neither parent is at home between 6.00am and 8.00am, at which times the children are left alone.

► Rajdeep is four years old. She is Asian and was born in India. Rajdeep has just started going to the reception class in her local school. She has not attended any school or early education setting in the United Kingdom before and is not settling in very well. She is aggressive with the other children and does not want to participate in some of the games and activities. The teacher talks to her parents about his concerns. That night Rajdeep is locked in her room with nothing to eat.

► Candy is an 11-month-old African-Caribbean baby. She has severe eczema all over her body. Her mum often doesn't use medicines or treatment given by the hospital, as she believes that through prayer and attendance at church Candy will get better.

► Simon is two and a half years old and is going through a phase of temper tantrums which sometimes cause him to lash out at other children, including his three-week-old sister. His mother believes in learning from example, so if Simon smacks his little sister she smacks him. Simon still hasn't learnt the lesson, so his mum has to smack him three or four times a day.

► Sam and Kimberley work together in the pre-school room in a nursery. Kimberley is unhappy about Sam's words and actions towards the children. Sam is keen to persist in tickling and wrestling games even when children say, 'Stop it'. A few of the children now appear to avoid Sam and go to Kimberley if they want help. Sam has also taken a definite dislike to two children in the group, calling them names like 'slowcoach' or 'peabrain'. Kimberley feels this behaviour goes against the centre behaviour policy because Sam is nagging and targeting the children in a negative way. Sam claims it is just a joke.

As you read on, think back to these scenarios, to your immediate reactions and thoughts. Would you respond differently once you know more about the issues?

Ideas for how to respond to each of these situations are given at the end of the chapter, on pages 11–13. These are based on the legal framework in relation to child protection and on the experience of people who have worked with children in similar situations.

2 Emotional abuse

Emotional abuse is the persistent emotional ill-treatment of a child, which causes severe and persistent adverse effects on the child's emotional development. Children may have been made to feel that they are worthless or unloved, inadequate or valued only insofar as they meet the needs of another person. Expectations that are inappropriate to a child's age or stage of development may have been imposed on them. The abuse may cause children to feel persistently frightened or in danger; it may exploit or corrupt them. Some level of emotional abuse is involved in all types of ill-treatment of a child, though it may occur alone.

3 Sexual abuse

Sexual abuse involves forcing or enticing a child to take part in sexual activities, whether or not the child is aware of what is happening. The activities may involve physical contact, including penetrative or non-penetrative acts. They may also include non-contact activities, such as involving children in looking at, or helping to produce, pornographic material, watching sexual activities or encouraging children to behave in sexually inappropriate ways.

4 Neglect

Neglect is the persistent failure to meet a child's basic physical and/or psychological needs, likely to result in the serious impairment of the child's health or development. It may involve a parent or carer failing to provide adequate food, shelter or clothing, failing to protect a child from physical harm or danger, or the failure to ensure access to appropriate medical care or treatment. It may also include neglect of, or failure to respond to, a child's basic emotional needs.

Bullying

Bullying is not an official category of abuse but it can cause significant harm to children. It is not always easy to define, but may be characterised by:
► deliberate hostility and aggression towards a person
► the victim being less powerful than the bully or bullies
► a painful and distressing outcome for the victim.

Types of bullying might include:
► physical pushing, kicking, hitting and pinching

► verbal name-calling, sarcasm, spreading of rumours, persistent teasing (disabled children are often particularly vulnerable here)
► emotional tormenting, ridicule, humiliation and continuous ignoring of individuals
► racial taunts, graffiti and gestures
► sexual and abusive comments and unwanted physical contact
► abusive telephone calls, text messages or emails.

Frequently asked questions

1 Do people really abuse very young children?

On 31 March 2001 there were 26,800 children on child protection registers in England. Of those, 30% were under four years (8,000 children), and more than 10% (2,800) were under a year old (Department of Health 2001a).

Children placed on a child protection register are considered to be at risk of abuse. [See 'Numbers on child protection registers', p. 16.]

2 Are most children abused by strangers?

No, most children are abused by someone they know and trust. This may be a family member, parent, aunt, uncle, brother, sister, childminder, nursery nurse or teacher. There are no statistics available to compare the number of children being abused in the home and the number abused by people who don't live with them, but we know that most children are abused at home because of what they tell us.

Children in the UK are more likely to be killed by a member of their family in their own home than by a stranger in a strange place (Brown & Lynch 1995). The homicide rate for children of a year old is nearly five times greater than the average, with 59 offences per million of the population of under-ones compared to 14 offences per million of the population as a whole (Home Office 2000a).

3 Is child abuse relevant to me?

Protecting children is everybody's responsibility. Children are the most vulnerable members of our society. Abuse of a child in your setting may seem highly unlikely, but when it does happen it can be devastating for everyone concerned.

Initiatives such as Sure Start and Quality Protects, and the general legal framework for child protection [see Appendix 1] show a move to early inter-agency work with families to identify their needs and ensure that they receive appropriate support. This is essential if we are to offer children effective protection and to promote the best outcomes for them and their families. Inquiries into the most serious cases of child abuse and child deaths have shown that people – neighbours, health care and education professionals – who noticed odd behaviour still thought it wasn't their business to get involved. Don't ever think 'it could never happen here' because children can be abused in any setting, by anyone.

4 Is smacking child abuse?

At the time of going to press, it is not illegal in the UK for parents to smack their children because the law allows them to administer 'reasonable chastisement'. This leaves the extent of physical punishment that parents may inflict on children open to interpretation. What sort of behaviour from a child might be thought to merit a smack? Does 'reasonable chastisement' imply a light tap on the back, a smack on the bottom, a slap around the face or a beating with a slipper, belt or stick? This confusion means that there is no clear guidance for parents or professionals, that each case has to be considered separately – and that the law leaves enough space for adults to inflict physical punishment that might otherwise be interpreted as cruelty.

The younger the child who is hit forcefully by an adult, the more vulnerable he is to serious injury or death through physical assault. Child deaths can occur as a result of a single incident or repeated lesser assaults:

▶ of all child deaths due to murder, about 40% occur during infancy (0–12 months), 20% during age 1–4 years and the remainder in the years up to age 15 (Creighton 1995)

▶ 50% of victims murdered by a parent or carer are aged 0–12 months (Brewster *et al.* 1998)

▶ 52% of one-year-olds are hit or 'smacked' once a week or more by their parents (Nobes *et al.* 1999).

The concern is that if a certain level of violence to children is acceptable, it is harder to draw the line and harder to know when to stop. This isn't to suggest that every parent who 'smacks' their child is inherently bad, but the potential consequences and risk of harming children physically and emotionally through 'smacking' need to be weighed against how effective it is, and how other strategies can produce more positive outcomes (Leach 1997a; 1997b).

In response, the policy position of both the NSPCC and the National Early Years Network is that the use of physical punishment against children – though sometimes understandable – is both unacceptable and ineffective, and should be ended by legal reform and public education. Legal reform should ensure that children have consistent protection against physical punishment in all settings outside the home, including private education and childminding facilities. These reforms should be accompanied by government-funded public education programmes on positive parenting that promote alternative forms of discipline.

Note that a change to the law on smacking in Scotland has been proposed by the Scottish Executive. If the proposals go ahead, it will be illegal in Scotland to smack a child under three, to hit any child on the head, to shake any child or use an implement to 'smack'. If the Bill goes through the Scottish Parliament, the proposals could become law by the end of 2002.

5 There are no men working in our nursery, so can we at least assume that children won't be at risk of abuse here?

The majority of convicted child sexual abusers that are known are male, but it is known that women may sexually abuse children. Many cases where women are alleged to sexually abuse are not reported or believed impossible. The need to be vigilant on children's behalf exists in all circumstances.

6 If I tell social services, will the children be taken away from home by interfering social workers?

Social workers have to work within laws and guidance which determine their roles, duties and responsibilities. At the forefront of their minds are the questions, 'How can I keep this child safe?', and 'What is best for this child?' In more than 90% of cases, the answer to both questions is to leave the child at home but to offer the family help and support, making sure the child is not at risk of abuse so the child can stay at home.

Sometimes, however, the circumstances at home pose such a risk to children that, as a last resort, they are removed for their own safety. If this happens, social workers generally try to identify family or friends where it is safe for the child to go and stay; most of these removals are only temporary.

7 Don't children often lie about abuse?

Children rarely lie about abuse. Their fear, and often their experience, is that people won't believe them. Children may make an allegation against someone that isn't true as a 'cry for help', because someone else is abusing them or something else is making them unhappy.

8 How can you tell if very young children are being abused?

Young children and some disabled children may have limited or no verbal communication. This makes them even more vulnerable, as abusers might think there is no way anyone will find out. An understanding of child development is very helpful in identifying and assessing child abuse, as development is often delayed in children who have not been able to form a strong relationship, or 'attachment' [see 'Relationships and attachment', p. 14], who are living in difficult circumstances [see 'Key problems' box, pp. 16–17] or who are being abused.

Think it over – some responses

The most difficult issue to understand is that there are no clear-cut answers to whether or not child abuse is taking place. The law is open to a great deal of interpretation, as is every single situation. All we can provide here are some pointers to help you consider the implications in each of the given scenarios. See page 8 for scenario outlines.

Scenario 1

Children rely on adults to protect them, and parents are responsible for making sure that their children are happy and well looked after in their absence. Sometimes it is difficult to find someone suitable to look after children – it can be expensive or difficult to find someone willing to be there for unusual hours. There is no set age at which it is acceptable to leave children home alone; it depends on an individual child's maturity, her ability to look after herself and cope in an emergency, and whether she feels happy about being left. The law does not say it is illegal for parents to leave their children alone, but parents can be prosecuted for wilful neglect if they leave a child unsupervised 'in a manner likely to cause unnecessary suffering or injury to health' (Children and Young Persons Act 1933).

The issues to consider in this scenario:
- Are Andrew and Suzy mature and confident enough to care for themselves, the twins and any emergency that might arise?
- Can they use the phone?
- Would they open the door to strangers?
- Who helps the twins get dressed, have breakfast, get to day care?
- How do Andrew and Suzy get to school?
- Is there a neighbour who is aware of them being alone and could help or be called in an emergency?

The children may not be left alone very often. How it may affect them depends upon the answers to the above. Neglect, as a form of abuse, is when a parent or carer *persistently* fails to meet a child's needs or *persistently* leaves her home alone. However, a single accident could have drastic consequences. The NSPCC leaflet *Home alone* is a good source that summarises this advice.

Scenario 2

Everyone has opinions about how children should behave, and parents can have difficulties and worries about making sure that their children achieve and do well. However, punishing children can have a negative impact on their self-esteem, confidence and understanding of what is right and wrong. Rajdeep's behaviour in school may not be simple 'naughtiness'.

There are several issues to consider in relation to this scenario.
- Is the behaviour intended to attract needed attention?
- Are there issues of difference, such as race, culture, language or religion that mean Rajdeep is being treated differently by the teachers and children in the school?
- Is there bullying or racism?
- Is Rajdeep frightened by being in a new situation, and in need of time and reassurance to adapt?
- Is her behaviour an indicator that she is being treated badly at home or being abused? [See Chapter 4.]
- How often is Rajdeep denied food or locked in a room?
- What does she usually experience in terms of attention, loving and caring relationships?

It is hard work for young children to learn the difference between what is acceptable behaviour and what is not. There are many good strategies to help them resolve differences, the simplest of these being to encourage and reward positive behaviour (see Finch 1998; Leach 1997a; 1997b).

A positive approach to dealing with Rajdeep's behaviour would be for her parents and the school to explore why she is unhappy and uncooperative. Listening to children means paying attention to what they say and encouraging them to share their thoughts and feelings.

Food and nourishment are essential for child growth and development. If parents withdraw something their child wants in order to encourage acceptable behaviour, it should be something that will make the child stop and think, but not cause her any harm or discomfort. It should also come as soon after the event as possible and should last for an appropriate amount of time according to the child's age and understanding. Young children only have a limited ability to remember events or rationalise severe punishments. Rajdeep may have experienced fear, hunger, anger, loss or confusion, and not have known why.

In terms of the law, social services would judge whether or not Rajdeep has suffered from abuse by interpreting (a) what constitutes 'significant harm' under the Children Act 1989 [see 'Section 47', p. 62] and (b) the legal defence of 'reasonable chastisement' when using physical means of disciplining a child.

[For more guidance, see emotional abuse and neglect under 'Categories of abuse', p. 9.]

Scenario 3

Everyone has beliefs and values, and parents have the right to raise children within their system of beliefs. At the same time, society has 'norms' and ideas about what is generally to be expected.

A child may be in need of protection if she has experienced, or is at risk of experiencing, 'significant harm'. This harm may be the impairment of health compared with what would usually be expected for similar children – in this case compared with the general outcomes for children with severe eczema. The issues to consider for this scenario are:

► What is the extent of Candy's condition?
► Is Candy experiencing pain and discomfort?
► Is there 'impairment of health' which could affect her development, *eg* the condition may cause sleep disturbances or restrict physical movement?

[For more guidance, see neglect under 'Categories of abuse', p. 9.]

Scenario 4

In the UK it is not illegal for parents to 'smack' their children because the law defends their right to 'reasonable chastisement' [see 'Is smacking child abuse', p. 10].

At the same time, the UK has agreed to abide by the rules of the United Nations Convention on the Rights of the Child. This states that children have the right to be protected from all forms of physical and mental violence and from deliberate humiliation. Consider the following questions:

► Does Simon understand why he is being smacked?
► Does Simon understand why smacking his sister is not OK?
► What is the difference between a smack, a slap, a tap and a whack?
► What is influencing Judy's stress levels?

Any form of physical violence towards a child can cause injury and be damaging to his emotional wellbeing. For young children a blow from an adult – especially around the head – can cause fatal injury. As mentioned in the response to Scenario 2, children do not always understand what they have done wrong. This is particularly true if a child has been smacked, because he might become too angry and upset to think clearly (see Hyder & Willow 1999).

For useful information, refer to two NSPCC leaflets: *Behave yourself* and *Encouraging better behaviour: a guide to positive parenting*.

Scenario 5

All adults have responsibilities to treat children with care and personal respect. There is no social, ethnic or professional group that we can say confidently would never treat children in an abusive way. So early years teams need to be ready to challenge poor or worrying practice from colleagues. Sam's behaviour is inappropriate and unpleasant. It needs to be challenged by Kimberley with the full support of the manager.

It is uncertain from the information in the scenario whether Sam's behaviour has crossed the border into possible sexual abuse through inappropriate contact. However, it is unacceptable to continue with close-contact physical games when children clearly wish to stop. Apart from failing to show children proper respect, it gives the risky message that adults have the right to demand physical contact regardless of children's preferences. Using negative labels for children is adult name-calling and is not a joke. Continued targeting of children by an adult can grow into an emotionally abusive situation that undermines the child's sense of self-worth.

Sam could be male or female. What sex did you assume that Sam was and in what ways may that have shaped your reaction to the scenario? The above comments apply equally to a male or female practitioner. Clear guidance needs to be given to Sam by the manager of the centre about physical and verbal respect for children. If Sam persists in these patterns of behaviour, even if there is no suspicion about actual abuse, the manager should consider the steps needed for disciplinary action.

2 Who abuses children?

Child abuse and neglect are terms used to describe ways in which children are harmed. It is usually adults who abuse children by inflicting harm or failing to prevent it, but children may also be abused by their siblings, cousins or 'friends'. Children are most often abused by people they know and trust: someone in their family, community or institution. It is rarer for a child to be abused by a stranger. So it is impossible to 'spot' a child abuser. They might be:

► parent, uncle, aunt, cousin, brother, sister or grandparent
► family friend or neighbour
► teenage babysitter or other child
► trusted adult (teacher, sports coach, youth worker, priest, scout/guide leader, respite carer, childminder, foster parent, friend's parent, nursery or playgroup worker, residential or field social worker).

People who abuse children cross all relationships, ages, classes, sexes, ethnicities, sexuality and disability.

Relationships and attachment

The development of relationships is fundamental to all human beings. Early, formative relationships have considerable influence on all aspects of human interaction, but especially on the ability to maintain positive relationships and to care successfully for children. A strong early relationship is known as an 'attachment', and much of the research in this area aims to understand what contributes to difficulties in forming this bond between parents and children (Elfer 1997; Rutter 1995). Early difficulties in a parent–child relationship may be forewarning of abuse or may even be a factor in causing it to happen. They may also affect a child's capacity to cope with abuse, as attachment helps children to:

► attain full intellectual potential
► understand their perceptions
► think logically
► develop a conscience
► become self-reliant
► cope with stress and frustration
► handle fear and worry
► develop future relationships
► feel less jealousy. (Fahlberg 1988; 1994.)

Lack of attachment is linked with problems such as:

► failure to develop a conscience
► lack of self-control
► low self-esteem
► poor interpersonal interactions
► inability to deal with emotions
► poor development of cognitive skills, such as understanding cause and effect and using logical thought
► behaviour difficulties
► slow development of gross and fine motor control and other skills.

There is an excellent book which examines how early years practitioners can respond to children whose development has been disrupted by traumatic events or abusive experiences (Daniel, Wassell & Gilligan 1999). It describes how each child is born with 'potential' and how a successful childhood can be seen in terms of reaching that potential. Some aspects of adult behaviour will support the development of potential, while others will inhibit it and some will have devastating effects. Understanding attachment does not simply help us protect children, it also promotes their welfare and potential.

Attachment applies not only to the parent–child relationship; a child needs healthy relationships with all significant adults and children, in many contexts. This is the guiding principle behind the development of the 'key person' system in early years care, in which a practitioner is identified as the main adult responsible for a child's care, education and welfare while attending a day care setting (Elfer, Goldschmied & Selleck 2002; Goldschmied & Jackson 1994). [For more on parenting style, see 'Support for families in need', pp. 54–5.]

Impact of stress on parents' ability to care

There are no absolute criteria on which to rely when judging what is 'significant harm' to children. There are many situations which can be seen as maltreatment, and many factors which may impact on a child's healthy development and welfare. The child and family's circumstances, including sources of stress, will inform an assessment about the degree of risk of significant harm and whether any professional support is required.

Family stress might be caused by something that is happening to the child (a period of illness, bullying by older children), the parent (unemployment, death of own parent) or the whole family (divorce, homelessness). Adults respond to stress in different ways; and how they respond can have an effect on their capacity to offer safe care to their children.

As an early years practitioner, knowledge of the issues that can affect parenting will help you encourage parents to seek help from the appropriate services, *eg* health, counselling, housing, police or legal advice. Your support could help parents make decisions that prioritise their child's welfare.

Advice and guidance about safety in the home, options for day care provision, health and hygiene, behaviour management techniques or children's developmental needs may all help a parent experiencing difficulties to provide a safe and secure environment for their child. You might also be able to help the child understand their home situation and develop ways of coping. All children – whether at risk or not – will benefit from careful guidance in how to seek out a trusted adult should there be trouble at home, and even call the police or other emergency services in times of danger. (See Lindon 2000 for advice on how to help children learn important lifeskills.)

In the end, the impact of stress on children depends largely on their resilience and temperament, their age and the positive parenting they receive. For useful information, refer to the NSPCC leaflet, *Stress: a guide for parents*.

Social exclusion

Many families suffer from multiple disadvantage. Some lack a wage earner, and poverty may mean that children live in crowded or unsuitable accommodation, have poor diets, health problems or disability, are vulnerable to accidents and lack ready access to good education or leisure opportunities. But beware of assuming that child abuse is more likely in disadvantaged communities. The majority of families living in poverty do not harm their children – and child abuse can happen in any context, whether disadvantaged or privileged.

Social exclusion is not just about poverty; discrimination may also be a factor [see 'Discrimination', right].

Mental illness, substance abuse and domestic violence

The problems that parents experience can have a damaging effect on their ability to meet their children's needs. Research shows that many children involved in the child protection system live, or have lived, in families where there are either high levels of parental mental illness, alcohol and drug abuse and/or violence in the family (Department of Health 1995). One study of suspected child abuse found that 'multi-problem' families (where more than one of these issues was present) made up 43% of the cases (Cleaver & Freeman 1995).

It is wrong to suggest that every child living with a parent who may experience these difficulties is at increased risk of abuse. However, if there is a significant level of one problem or a combination of mental illness, substance abuse and/or violence, the impact on children may have long-term harmful effects.

The development and emotional wellbeing of children who see, hear or become caught up in violence in the home can be seriously affected. Pre-school children are more likely to display physical symptoms of their anxiety, such as stomach aches, bed-wetting, sleeping difficulties, diarrhoea and asthma (Hester, Pearson & Harwin 1998; 2000). The adult who is the victim of violence may find it more difficult to provide appropriate care and parenting. [For guidance on legal protection against domestic violence, see 'Family Law Act 1996', pp. 64–5.]

When parents' ability to care is affected by mental illness, substance abuse, and/or violence, the age of the child will influence how they may be affected (Cleaver, Unell & Aldgate 1999) [see 'Key problems' box, pp. 16–17].

Discrimination

Individuals and families may experience discrimination or harassment because they are 'different', perhaps as a result of poverty, disability, sexual orientation, housing conditions, religion or ethnicity.

Where discrimination is a result of racism, the question is not *if* it will adversely affect children, but *how* it will do so (Macdonald 1991). Not only are black and minority ethnic families' needs for services not always well met (Butt & Mirza 1996), misunderstandings over cultural practices and ineffective support for people whose first language is not English can cause additional stress for families who

Key problems for children living with parents' mental illness, substance abuse and domestic violence

Children aged 0–2 years

- Drug and alcohol use during pregnancy may have caused neurological and physical damage.
- Children can be physically and emotionally neglected, to the detriment of their health.
- Children may be subjected to direct physical violence by parents.
- Health problems may be exacerbated by living in an impoverished environment.
- Cognitive development may be delayed through parents' inconsistent, under-stimulating and neglectful behaviour.
- Children may fail to develop a positive identity because they are rejected and are uncertain of who they are.
- Babies suffering from withdrawal symptoms from foetal addiction may be difficult to manage.
- A lack of commitment and increased unhappiness, tension and irritability in parents may make it more difficult for the child to form an attachment [see 'Relationships and attachment, p. 14].
- Children are placed in physical danger, eg through lack of supervision or having access to dangerous substances, by parents whose physical capacity to care is impaired or limited.
- Attachment may be damaged by inconsistent parenting.

- Children may be at risk because they are unable to tell anybody about their distress.

Children aged 3–4 years

The problems listed above, plus the following:
- Cognitive development may be delayed through lack of stimulation, disorganisation and failure to attend pre-school facilities.
- Children may learn inappropriate behaviour through witnessing domestic violence.
- When parents' behaviour is unpredictable and frightening, children may display emotional symptoms similar to those of post-traumatic stress disorder.
- Children may take on responsibilities beyond their years because of parental incapacity.

Factors that can protect children aged 0–4 years
- The presence of another caring adult who can respond to the child's developmental needs.
- Sufficient income and good physical standards in the home.
- Regular supportive help from a primary health care team and social services, including consistent day care.
- An alternative safe and supportive residence for parents subject to violence and the threat of violence.

---

become involved in child protection investigations (Farmer & Owen 1995).

But difference can also hide abuse, because people may miss the signs. A child who is living in dreadful housing conditions may always be dirty and smelly, and practitioners will almost certainly try to encourage other children to show caring and empathy towards the child's difficult living circumstances. But what if the poor housing conditions are not the whole story? There is a world of difference between a child whose parents are attempting to create a loving home despite losing the battle against poor sanitation, and a child whose parents abuse him in those surroundings. The fact that a child is dirty could lead a caring adult to miss a deeper problem.

As in all things related to child abuse, it's important to know as much as possible before drawing any conclusions.

Extent of child abuse

Nobody can be sure how many children are being abused or if the numbers are rising or falling. After all, it was only in the late 20th century that society came to accept that child sexual abuse exists at all, let alone consider the lasting effects it can have on children and their relationships as adults (Jones & Ramchandani 1999). What we do know is that most children lead happy, safe lives – and that far more children than ever are receiving help and support from professionals working in the field.

Numbers on child protection registers
The Department of Health emphasises that local authority child protection registers are not intended to list all children who have been abused and come to official notice. They are instead intended to protect individual

Children aged 5–8 years

▶ Children may be at increased risk of physical injury and show symptoms of extreme anxiety and fear.
▶ School work may suffer and children's behaviour in school could become problematic. Boys tend to exhibit problem behaviour more quickly, but girls' behaviour and achievement are also affected if parental problems continue.
▶ Children may develop poor self-esteem and blame themselves for their parents' problems.
▶ Inconsistent parental behaviour may cause anxiety and difficulty with attachment.
▶ Children may develop an extreme fear of hostility.
▶ Unplanned separation can cause distress, and disrupt education and friendship patterns.
▶ Children may feel embarrassed and ashamed about their parents' behaviour, and so limit friendships and social interaction.
▶ Children may take on too much responsibility for themselves, their parents and their siblings.

Factors that can protect children aged 5–8 years

As for children aged 0–4 years, plus the following.

▶ An ability to think of drug and alcohol problems as illnesses, enabling children to accept and cope with parents' behaviour more easily.
▶ Regular attendance at school.
▶ Sympathetic and vigilant teachers.
▶ Attendance at school medicals.
▶ A supportive older sibling; older siblings can be very significant, particularly when parents are overwhelmed by their own problems (Kosonen 1996).
▶ A friend; children who have at least one mutual friend have higher self-esteem and lower scores on loneliness than those without (Stocker 1994).
▶ Social networks outside the family, especially with a sympathetic adult of the same sex.
▶ Belonging to organised out-of-school activities, including homework clubs.
▶ Being taught different ways of coping and being sufficiently confident to know what to do when parents are incapacitated.
▶ An ability to distance oneself either psychologically or physically from the stressful situation.

---

children from significant harm in the future by ensuring that there is a child protection plan in place. At the extreme end this means that a child who has died as a result of abuse in the family will not appear on the local authority register, but any surviving siblings will probably be listed.

Registers are not static. Children are added to child protection registers ('registered') as they are considered to need protection, and removed from them ('deregistered') when they no longer need it.

On 31 March 2001 there were 26,800 children on child protection registers in England (Department of Health 2001a). Because the registers list only those children for whom a child protection plan is in place, they do not represent all cases of child abuse, nor even those reported (or referred) to child protection agencies. It has been estimated that only one in seven of the children referred

to English local authorities is finally registered (Gibbons, Conroy & Bell 1995). Referrals are filtered out in the course of the child protection investigation [see Chapter 8].

In Scotland, in the year ending 31 March 1999, there were around 7,300 children referred for child protection inquiries; 2,734 of the referrals went to initial child protection case conferences. Of these, 1,962 children were placed on child protection registers (one in approximately every four referrals).

Children referred to child protection agencies and subsequently added to child protection registers are drawn disproportionately from socially disadvantaged families. While these families suffer more from the internal and external factors which have an impact on adults' ability to care and which are therefore associated with child abuse (see 'Impact of stress on parents' ability to care', pp. 14–16), they are also subject to more social surveillance and may need support even if child protection services are not required. All the research evidence suggests that enhancing children's wider quality of life increases the likelihood of protection from abuse (Department of Health 1995, p. 49).

Child maltreatment

There are no national statistics showing the extent of the different categories of child abuse. However, some estimates have been made using research studies on representative samples of the general public (usually adult), asking about their childhood experiences. The following statistics on prevalence of child abuse are drawn from an important study into child maltreatment (Cawson et al. 2000).

A nationally representative sample of 2,869 young adults aged 18–24 was asked about their childhood experiences of abusive physical, sexual, neglectful and emotional maltreatment within the family home.

- Serious physical abuse was defined as: 'All those children who had regularly experienced violent treatment at the hands of their parents or carers, or had received injuries as a result of such treatment, or which frequently led to physical effects lasting until the next day.' Seven per cent (7%) reported that they had experienced childhood physical abuse.

- Child sexual abuse was defined as: 'Sexual acts to which they have not consented or when they were aged 12 or less.' One per cent (1%) of the sample said they had been sexually abused by a parent or carer, with a further 2% reporting abuse by a relative. Most of those reporting sexual abuse were women and the overwhelming majority of such experiences had involved physical contact.

- The analysis of all childhood experiences of sexual abuse (ie all experiences of abuse, whether at the hands of a family member or someone else) revealed that 16% of the sample experienced abuse, with 11% of incidents involving physical contact. Girls were more likely to have been sexually abused than boys and 6% of the sample said that they had regarded it as abusive.

- Six per cent (6%) of the sample reported childhood neglect, and nearly 6% reported emotional abuse.

3 Impact of child abuse

Many factors will influence the effect that abuse has on a child. You've almost certainly heard people say, 'Well I was hit as a child and it didn't do me any harm'. But the impact on children of being hit depends on several factors, such as:

► how many times they are hit
► with what
► how much pain is suffered or injury incurred
► whether they usually receive positive love and warmth (see, for example, Larzelere 2000).

For many children, continuous abuse can have major long-term effects on all aspects of their health, development and wellbeing. Sustained abuse is likely to have a deep impact on a child's self-image and self-esteem, and these difficulties may continue into adulthood, perhaps affecting a person's relationships, confidence in the workplace or parenting style. This does not mean that everyone who has been abused as a child will be negatively affected as an adult, but many children who experience abuse need help and support to help them grow into emotionally healthy and successful adults.

Many adults who were abused as children say that the first step to healing was telling someone, and being listened to and believed. Your response and the responses of other professionals can affect how that child feels and understands the abuse, now and later.

Resilience

Many children live in extremely difficult family circumstances but overcome these to become fully developed, well-adjusted adults – and the vast majority of parents living in difficult circumstances are able to give their children the love and emotional support they need (Cleaver, Unell & Aldgate 1999). Furthermore, most children living in difficult circumstances receive positive input, support and care, not only from their parents but also from relatives, friends and the wider community. This support can mean that the child and/or family do not need assistance from social services.

A child can also build resilience, or strength, which counteracts the impact of

---

> ## Impact of abuse
>
> ### Physical abuse
> Death, injury and pain, disability, neurological damage, aggressive behaviour, emotional and behavioural difficulties, educational difficulties.
>
> ### Emotional abuse
> Negative effect on the child's mental health, behaviour and self-esteem. Damage can be especially destructive if a child is abused in infancy.
>
> ### Sexual abuse
> Inappropriate sexual behaviour, self-harm, depression, traumatic flashbacks, low self-esteem. The longer-term impact of sexual abuse can be reduced if children have non-abusing adults who believe them (though this is complicated in the case of very young children who are not able to understand or communicate what is happening). Disabled children, particularly those with communication difficulties, have additional problems to overcome [see Chapter 5].
>
> ### Neglect
> Severe neglect can seriously affect the growth, health and intellectual development of young children. This can lead to difficulties with physical wellbeing, social functioning, relationships and educational progress. In extreme cases children can be seriously impaired or can die from neglect.

---

harm (and may even 'possess' resilience as a personal quality). Sometimes it is this which helps the child through and is one of the reasons why the impact of abuse can be so varied. This does not mean that a child should be left to be harmed, but it may affect the assessment and the action that child protection agencies might take.

Impact on individuals, families, groups and communities

The discovery of child abuse is shocking, whatever the circumstances. People may feel a range of emotions including guilt, anger, disgust, disbelief and betrayal, especially when the abuser is someone that they know and trust. Feelings of relief or justification may also emerge if someone had suspected abuse. For any group it might mean people are divided about their allegiances and whom they can trust.

If abuse has occurred within the family, individuals or sections of the family may be excluded or put under pressure to act in particular ways. Family members as well as the child may need support and reassurance through the process of the investigation, and beyond. If the abuser is a figure in the community, such as a teacher or a religious leader, whole communities can be affected. The impact can be particularly difficult to cope with when child protection investigations do not identify abuse, as families are unlikely to receive further input from social services (Gibbons 1991). This can result in children, families and early years practitioners feeling angry, confused and violated by the system.

It has been suggested that some of the responsibility for this oversight lies in the way that social workers tend to be too narrowly focused on child abuse, too defensive in their practices and unable to recognise that children's needs and standards of care are inextricably linked with their wider family situation (Corby 2000). However, social services are not designed to provide support to every family, and limitations on social services resources may mean that only children at risk of significant harm, or with a disability, are likely to receive social services' support.

As a consequence, practitioners working in day care or early education might be vital in promoting children's safety, welfare and best interests. Advice and support to a parent experiencing difficulties in managing their child's behaviour may be best given by the child's key person in a nursery setting rather than a social worker. The nursery can provide support and encouragement over time, without what some might perceive as the stigma of social services or the complexity of a relationship with a social worker who has undertaken a child protection investigation. Receiving support through statutory services such as education and health may enable a family to cope without any involvement of social services. It is an approach used by many family centres (Lloyd 1996; Smith 1996), and is behind initiatives like Sure Start and Early Excellence Centres.

4 Signs and indicators of abuse

Recognising abuse is not easy. It is *not* your responsibility to decide whether or not abuse has taken place, but if you feel there is cause for concern you can play a vital role by contacting social services, who can investigate and take any necessary action to protect a child. Never take any action without consulting others. [See Chapters 6, 7 and 9.]

The signs and indicators of abuse in this chapter form a general guide to visible impacts of abuse on children. They should not be interpreted as conclusive evidence of abuse, only as signs which might alert you to the need for closer observation or investigation. Other possible causes of injury or changes in behaviour should always be considered.

As someone who works with children you may at some point become concerned that one of them is being, or has been, abused. Young children may not have the language with which to talk about their experiences or the cognitive awareness to understand that they are being maltreated – which makes it all the more difficult to judge whether or not they are being abused.

With young children, one of the main indicators of abuse is its impact on their development. Early years practitioners already know the importance of identifying milestones in children's physical, cognitive and emotional development in order to track their progress. These very same markers of development – or rather their lack – can help identify children who are being abused.

But many other factors can affect a child's development (disability that has not yet been diagnosed, upheaval at home, grief at the death of a parent), and it is vital to know as much as possible about a child's home life and environment before making any judgement on the likely causes of developmental delay. Good record-keeping and observation in an early years setting can provide essential reference material for the experts who eventually make that judgement.

Identifying when a child is *not* being abused

Practitioners can play a key role in protecting young children simply by gathering information about all the children in their care, so that contact and work with them is child-focused and appropriate to each child's needs. Good information also helps avoid misinterpretation of something benign as a sign of abuse. For instance, at one time black children who had a 'Mongolian blue spot' (a harmless birthmark that can appear on the lower back of any child but which is more common in children with darker skin) were often referred to social services by white professionals because they thought it was a bruise or injury. A simple query to all parents about their children's birthmarks or identifying features avoids this kind of misunderstanding.

While there is a range of ways in which children genuinely experience harm, there may be legitimate reasons to account for an injury or for children behaving in certain ways. A routine exchange of information with parents about illness, injury or changes in behaviour will help you judge what is really going on. Medical conditions such as eczema can sometimes look like physical injury, and records of a child's medical history will help avoid confusion (though do beware – an adult who is abusing a child may use a medical condition as an excuse to cover up injuries that have actually been caused through abuse).

Bruising may be more or less noticeable on children with different skin tones, from different racial groups or with some medical conditions.

- Black practitioners may think that the vivid bruising of white skin is more serious than it really is.
- Some blood conditions, including haemophilia, result in the skin bruising much more easily and more severely than would usually be expected.
- 'Brittle bone' syndrome exposes children to frequent bone fractures that may look deliberately inflicted, but may be genuinely accidental.

Differences in cultural practices may cause children to behave in unexpected ways. For example, at one nursery a four-year-old Asian Muslim girl became very distressed and refused to get undressed for water play. Staff felt this was unusual and were concerned that it could be a sign that she was being abused. In fact the girl's family culture did not include water play, swimming or even bathing. The family always used a bucket as a shower-type way of washing. The girl was scared and had never experienced water play or anyone other than her family undressing her. Knowledge of the religion and cultural practices of children attending an early years setting will help practitioners plan appropriate activities, and this is most effectively achieved if the staff mirrors the ethnic and cultural balance of the children.

Disabled children also need special consideration when identifying indicators of abuse. They may have personal care needs, medical conditions or equipment aids which should be taken into account when identifying indicators of abuse. Also consider a disabled child's communication skills, which may be different from those you are familiar with. Disabled children are often treated 'differently' from non-disabled children, and they are more likely to spend time in residential care or have multiple carers (NSPCC *et al.* 1993).

Physical abuse

Most children will collect cuts and bruises in their daily life. These are likely to be in places where there are bony parts of their body such as elbows, knees and shins. Their age, physical mobility and lifestyle (for instance whether they do lots of outdoor physical activities) will affect how many bumps and bruises they collect in a normal week or month.

An important indicator of physical abuse is where bruises or injuries are unexplained or appear on parts of the body where accidental injuries are unlikely, for example on the cheeks or thighs. However, accidental injuries, which might normally be ignored, could also be a sign of inappropriate supervision if they happen frequently.

Any regular reports given by siblings, friends or neighbours about bullying or physical injury must be taken seriously. Any delay by parents in seeking medical treatment where necessary is also a cause for concern. Severe physical injury to young children can cause permanent harm including brain damage, disability, and death.

It is useful to note that children who have been physically harmed are sometimes purposefully kept away from day care and early education to allow the injuries to heal and therefore go undetected.

Signs and indicators of possible physical abuse

Under one year old
Any bruising, especially:
► small circular bruises to facial area – could indicate fingers gripping the face
► injuries to the mouth – might be a sign of non-accidental injury through force-feeding; this may be indicated by bruising to both sides of the mouth or cheeks, or by internal mouth injuries
► bruises to cheeks, ears and forehead following blows with the flat of a hand
► finger-shaped bruising around the width of a limb caused by an excessively tight grip
► finger bruising of the trunk, which may indicate gripping in order to shake the child; this is potentially dangerous and must always be taken seriously
► many bruises at different stages of healing – could indicate repeated injury.

Other injuries and skin marks, especially burns or bites:
► sadistic injuries include cigarette burns, holding against a fireguard and deliberate scalding (with any burn or scald, special attention should be paid to the history and context of the injury and to whether the explanation is plausible)
► bites, including animal bites
► swelling and unusual use of limbs
► injuries inside the mouth – of particular concern in bottle-fed babies
► any serious injury with no explanation, or with conflicting explanations
► untreated injuries.

More severe injuries, especially fractures:
► fractures should always be considered as possibly indicative of significant harm in this age group, and medical advice should always be sought
► brain injury – signs may include drowsiness, vomiting or fits; this may be the result of the child being physically shaken or hit
► cot death (Sudden Infant Death Syndrome) – circumstances should always be sympathetically explored; all cot deaths are investigated by the police, but do not automatically require joint child protection procedures to be initiated.

One to eight years
In addition to the signs listed for 'Under one year old', above, be alert to changes in behaviour which can indicate physical abuse:

- hyper-vigilance and watchfulness
- flinching when approached or touched, especially in response to a particular carer
- withdrawn behaviour
- depression
- running away
- fear of going home
- fear of parents being contacted
- reluctance to get changed, for example in hot weather
- aggressive behaviour or unusually severe temper outbursts.

It is vital to know the children in your care well, as many younger children may display some of these behaviours as part of their expected development. Is their behaviour constant? Does it ever seem worse or better? If so, what has influenced this change? Child abuse should be *one* of the causes you consider; it should not be the only explanation. Some of the changes in behaviour could have harmless causes, for example some children are aggressive towards younger children following the birth of a sibling.

Generally, though, children's behaviour is a good indicator of their health and wellbeing. If children are unhappy or afraid they may either demand more attention or isolate themselves. Children who flinch away from normal contact with you (for example, when you are touching their arm to attract attention) may have been hit regularly.

Fabricated or induced illness in children by carers

Parents or carers with a condition known as Factitious Illness by Proxy, or Munchausen Syndrome by Proxy, will feign the symptoms of or deliberately cause ill-health to a child they are looking after. This might be because the adult enjoys or needs the sympathetic attention they receive as a result of their child being ill.

The problem may be more complex when children have an illness, disorder or disability. A child may be given regular medication by a carer for genuine reasons and need regular health appointments for treatment. In such a case, fabricated or induced illness in the child may be masked by real health needs.

Fabricated or induced illness in children is included in the official definition of physical abuse, so it is important to be aware of this rare form of abuse because it can result in fatalities or serious long-term impairment. It is a complicated area, and both social services and health professionals have special arrangements for dealing sensitively with the issue, so it is essential that you consult and work together with them. The Department of Health has recently produced guidelines for agencies who may encounter this syndrome (Department of Health 2001b).

Emotional abuse

Emotional abuse can be difficult to measure, and often children who appear physically well cared for may be emotionally abused by being taunted and belittled or by receiving little or no love, affection or attention.

Signs and indicators of possible emotional abuse

Under one year old
- Frozen watchfulness – as the name suggests, this is where children will become still and withdraw but stay 'on guard' from a fear of violence, reprimand or punishment. Some research suggests that even very young babies will do this (Hague *et al.* 1996).
- Failure to thrive or grow, particularly if the child puts on weight in circumstances away from home, *eg* in hospital.
- Slow responses to stimulation – this may be early evidence of developmental delay, either in terms of physical or emotional progress.
- Poor interaction with main carer or parent.
- Self-stimulation, such as rocking or head banging.
- Babies who are shouted at may cry when picked up, preferring to be left in peace.
- An anxious baby may not feed well and sleep is fitful.

One to five years
- Indifference to the parent, passive acceptance of a change of carers or being over-affectionate.
- Temper tantrums or prolonged crying – perhaps a result of inconsistent management.
- Behaviour to attract attention or indiscriminate affection towards adults.
- Extreme sulking, *ie* not responding to positive attention.
- Self-stimulation such as hair twisting or rocking.
- Being unable to play.
- Being unable to make friends.
- Fear of making mistakes.
- Sudden speech disorders.
- Self-harm.
- Fear of parent being contacted.

Six to eight years
- ▶ Behaviour disorders – petty theft, telling lies, disruption of class in school, lack of response to discipline.
- ▶ Poor self-image, lack of confidence and insecurity.
- ▶ Lethargy and depression – tiredness, loss of vitality, decreased performance at school.
- ▶ Absenteeism, repeated lateness or running away.
- ▶ Wetting or soiling.

Sexual abuse

Both girls and boys can be abused by adults who may use children to meet their own sexual needs through sexual intercourse, masturbation, oral sex or fondling. Showing pornographic photographs or videos is also a form of sexual abuse.

Children from the ages of 0–17 years can experience sexual abuse. At 31 March 1999 there were approximately 360 infants under one year old who either had been or were at risk of sexual abuse.

Usually, in cases of sexual abuse it is the child's behaviour which may cause concern, although physical signs can also be present. With younger infants and babies it is more difficult to identify behaviour that explicitly indicates sexual abuse, but their young age does not mean that they will be protected from it. In all cases, children who tell about sexual abuse do so because they want it to stop, so it is important to listen and take them seriously.

Younger children who have experienced sexual abuse may have accepted sexual activity as part of 'normal' life. They might not have the cognitive development to understand what it is or that it is wrong. Sexual arousal in young children can be developed to a degree that is distressing for adults to deal with. It is important to seek guidance and support in dealing with sexually abused children and in how you respond to them.

Signs and indicators of possible sexual abuse
A child who is the victim of sexual abuse may behave in a sexually inappropriate way, showing the sexual awareness of an adult and initiating sexual games, either with other children or through masturbation. This behaviour is quite distinctive and should not be confused with masturbation for comfort or with the exploratory sexual games which many children engage in.

Under one year old
- ▶ Injury, pain or itching in the genital area.
- ▶ Bruising or bleeding near the genital area.
- ▶ Sexually transmitted disease – oral or vaginal.
- ▶ Vaginal discharge or infection.
- ▶ Unusual fear during particular situations, *eg* nappy changing.

One to five years
- ▶ Sexual knowledge that is beyond their age or developmental level, including descriptions of sexual experiences or observations.
- ▶ Sexual drawings or language.
- ▶ Sexual play with peers or toys.
- ▶ Genital injury.
- ▶ Vaginal discharge, bleeding, itching or soreness.
- ▶ Discomfort when walking or sitting down.
- ▶ Sexually transmitted disease – oral or vaginal.
- ▶ Physical harm associated with sexual abuse – bruises, bite marks or burns in the genital or lower abdominal area.

Six to eight years
As for 'One to five years', above, and:
- ▶ sudden or unexplained changes in behaviour, *eg* becoming aggressive or withdrawn
- ▶ fear of one person or particular people
- ▶ running away from home
- ▶ having nightmares
- ▶ bedwetting (where the child has not wet the bed for some time)
- ▶ eating problems such as obesity, anorexia or failure to thrive
- ▶ self-harm or mutilation (this is usually associated with older children and assumed to be extreme behaviour, but younger children can cause self-harm through pulling out hair, severe scratching, biting themselves, burns and scalds)
- ▶ saying they have secrets they cannot tell anyone about
- ▶ substance or drug abuse – even children eight and under might acquire and use alcohol or drugs, although it is more common in older children
- ▶ sudden unexplained sources of money
- ▶ taking over a parental role at home – under-eights have been known to behave in this way, especially if they are trying to protect younger siblings from their own experiences
- ▶ having no friends
- ▶ telling about the abuse.

Neglect

Neglect is a difficult form of abuse to recognise but it can have some of the most lasting and damaging effects on children.

Neglect can be perceived physically as poor standards of cleanliness, physical care or hygiene, infection and infestation. Children who are neglected or emotionally deprived often fail to thrive even in the absence of any specific medical condition. A child who seems unusually small should be monitored. There may be a perfectly normal explanation – one or both of the parents may be of slight build – but it may be a symptom of chronic neglect. Loss of appetite in a child may also be significant.

Signs and indicators of possible neglect

Under one year old
- Loss of weight, or being constantly underweight.
- Being significantly overweight.
- Arriving at day care wearing nappies which appear not to have been changed overnight.
- Untreated nappy rash.
- A baby who is constantly dirty or 'smelly'.
- Dehydration – babies cannot help themselves to a drink.
- A baby who is quiet and apathetic.
- Poor skin or hair tone.

One to eight years
As for 'Under one year old', above, and:
- constant hunger, sometimes stealing food from other children
- being tired all the time
- obsessive or anxious behaviour
- few friends
- frequent lateness or non-attendance
- destructive tendencies
- lack of confidence
- not seeking or expecting comfort or attention
- inappropriate dress – such as inadequate warm clothing in the winter
- consistent failure to attend the GP, health visitor, dentist, optician or hospital for any medical appointments.

Key messages about the signs of abuse

1 *The lists given above are not exhaustive.*
2 *Always consider the bigger picture.*

Many children and young people will exhibit some of the indicators listed above at some time, and the presence of one or more should never be taken as proof of abuse.

Always consult the child protection procedures where you work and consult the appropriate person who has responsibility for child protection in your setting. There are some indicators which are more significant than others:

- repeated unexplained injuries or unlikely explanations of 'accidents', *eg* a three year old with facial bruising but none to arms or legs who keeps 'falling down the stairs' – this child may not be being supervised properly (carers may not be using stair gates effectively) or may be at risk of serious physical harm from being hit or getting caught in violence between adults
- unexplained genital injury, signs of trauma or discharge
- limp or immobile limbs in infants that have not received treatment.

A badly abused or neglected child may show all these signs at once. Sexual and physical abuse nearly always include some form of emotional abuse and many children who are physically abused may also be neglected.

A child who experiences emotional harm may be affected in various ways, depending on personality, experience, class, ethnicity, culture and gender.

There may well be other reasons for changes in behaviour, such as a death or crisis in the family or the birth of a child. Your knowledge of a child over a period of time will help you understand whether there is at least some cause for you to be concerned.

How a child might 'tell'

Children communicate in many ways, not always by speech. How they do so depends on:
- their stage of development
- the language they are exposed to in formative years
- speech impairment or communication difficulty
- whether they have received an appropriate response to attempts to communicate (for example, if a child asks a question and is ignored she may do something to attract attention another way or might just stop asking questions).

A child who wants to communicate that something is wrong will probably approach someone he feels he can trust. Listening to children is not just about hearing the words they say – their communication may not be verbal or their actions may belie their words – so be aware of changes in a child's behaviour and attitude too. A child's developmental stage will influence how he hears words, and he may use them out of context. A seven-year-old child may say 'we shagged' but, when asked what that means, may describe holding hands and kissing (though if a child is persistently describing activities using sexually explicit language, drawings or play beyond his developmental stage and/or chronological age, this may be an indicator of concern). A child's developmental stage shapes his perception of events around him, including the concept of time.

Be aware of how a child's culture or lifestyle will affect how he communicates. It is good practice to have members of staff who mirror the ethnic and cultural mix of the children, and in this case a proportion of staff members can easily tune in to a child's method of communication.

The government has consistently emphasised the need to consult meaningfully with all children. To do so, you need to avoid words and activities that are beyond their developmental level and use their own communication system.

How children are silenced

Research has shown that many children never tell about abuse, and there are significant reasons for this. Children may be silenced if they are told that:

- their families, loved ones or pets will be hurt
- they will receive presents or treats
- they will be taken away from their family
- the abuse is normal – it happens to everyone
- it is their fault – they are bad
- no one will believe them if they tell
- the abuser will have to go to prison
- abuse is against their religion or belief – it cannot happen
- the abuse is happening because their belief in their religion is not strong enough.

Why adults don't hear

Child abuse is highly emotive, and sometimes adults fail to recognise that a child may be in need of protection. This may be because the child communicates in a way the adult does not understand, or because the adult thinks that:

- no one could possibly abuse a child in that way
- the child is too young, or not clever, and therefore is not trustworthy
- the child is a liar or is fantasising
- the child is wicked and evil
- the child is trying to get the adult into trouble
- no one would stoop so low as to abuse a disabled child.

5 Disabled children

The available evidence in the UK suggests that children with disabilities are at increased risk of abuse and that those with multiple disabilities are at an even greater risk of both abuse and neglect.

Many children with special educational needs and disabilities are unable to communicate verbally, and even those who can speak may rely more heavily than other children on physical contact, gesture or signing to assist their communication. Some children with physical disabilities need extensive support for intimate aspects of daily life and it may be difficult for them to distinguish what is acceptable and unacceptable behaviour towards them.

There are many other reasons why disabled children might be at greater risk. They may:

▶ have fewer outside contacts than other children

▶ receive intimate personal care, possibly from a number of carers, which may increase the risk of exposure to abusive behaviour and make it more difficult to set and maintain physical boundaries

▶ have an impaired capacity to resist or avoid abuse

▶ have communication difficulties that could make it difficult to tell others what is happening

▶ be inhibited about complaining because of a fear of losing services

▶ be especially vulnerable to bullying and intimidation

▶ be more vulnerable than other children to abuse by their peers.

Spontaneous disclosures of abuse in young children with disabilities are rare. Even if a child has some spoken language, she may not know the specific vocabulary to use. Signs of possible abuse may be seen in subtle changes in a child's behaviour or emotional state, such as displaying consistent unease or anxiety when being cared for by a particular person. Acting in a sexual way which is inappropriate to the child's age, whether in gestures or movements, may be a sign of sexual abuse.

Safeguarding disabled children

Safeguards for children with disabilities are essentially the same as for non-disabled children. Practitioners must be aware of the risks to disabled children and be committed to enabling children and families to help themselves.

It is also essential to understand an individual child's communication signals, especially her means of indicating 'yes' and 'no', and new carers might find it helpful if the child keeps a communication book which lists these methods of communication.

Measures to safeguard children with disabilities include the following:

▶ make it common practice to help disabled children express their wishes and feelings in respect of their care and treatment

▶ ensure that disabled children receive appropriate personal, health and social education, including awareness of their bodies and human relationships

▶ make sure that all disabled children know how to raise concerns if they are worried or angry about something, and give them access to a range of adults with whom they can communicate

▶ ensure that children with communication difficulties have access to all means of being heard

▶ anyone providing services used by disabled children must have an explicit commitment to, and understanding of, the safety and welfare of *all* children

▶ maintain close contact with families as part of a culture of openness

▶ establish guidelines and provide training for staff on:
  - good practice in intimate care
  - working with children of the opposite sex
  - handling difficult behaviour
  - consent to treatment
  - anti-bullying strategies.

Any investigation process should prepare the child for possible interviews: a trusted adult should explain clearly and carefully what will take place and act on the child's behalf, as appropriate. Preparation for the adults who take on this role will also be necessary so that they are clear of their role and responsibilities in relation to the investigation. It will take time for adults and child to develop ways of working where the child is given the power to communicate effectively in an interview situation.

Issues for parents and practitioners

Anyone working with a child who has a disability such as severe low vision will need to develop strategies that involve closer physical contact than when they are working with a fully sighted child. The child may need guiding or physical prompting; skills that a sighted child learns through visual imitation may need to be specifically taught through touch. The use of a physical prompt is often an essential stage when a disabled child is learning a new skill and should be used wherever necessary. It is, however, good practice to fade out such prompts as soon as the skill can be used independently.

It is important to discuss the nature of this contact with the child prior to any physical support, to alert the child to any contact and to seek the agreement of the child. Very young disabled children will need that information provided in a way that suits their stage of development.

For children with additional complex needs, therapies including massage form a very important part of their sensory curriculum. The following issues should be addressed in order that practitioners can apply these techniques sensitively:

▶ the setting should have an explicit policy of involving and empowering children
▶ parents and practitioners should feel confident to speak on a child's behalf if they suspect that he is unhappy about the way he is being handled
▶ doors to therapy rooms, light stimulation rooms or bedrooms should never be locked
▶ the setting's manager, all practitioners and parents should be aware of the purpose and frequency of any strategies or therapies that are used
▶ all strategies should be planned and recorded as part of the child's individual care plan, clearly indicating their aim and the adults to be involved.

Restraint

When disabled children display unsafe behaviour that may result in harm to themselves, it is vital to balance the risks of taking action to restrain them against the risks of *not* taking that action. The most important factor here is the welfare of the child. Training should be provided in safe and effective techniques for restraining a child with disabilities where the risk of harm is assessed as unacceptable.

6 Is Nathan at risk? Case study 1

This case study and the one in Chapter 9 give you an opportunity to read about the detailed process in deciding whether or not a child is at risk, and what happens along the way. The cases are examples of good practice that will inform your own practice and policymaking. They also offer some opportunities to think about what you would do in the given situation. What might cause you to be concerned and what might happen next? You can study this material on your own or with colleagues, and look at it during one or two sessions – or several. Don't worry about coming up with the 'wrong' responses; this is a safe way to think about what you know and believe, and how you can fulfil your role in protecting the children you help to look after.

The initial situation

Nathan Miller, aged three years (child)
Sara Miller, aged 21 years (mother)
Shirelle Miller, aged 18 years (aunt)
Joyce Miller, aged 65 years (grandmother)

Nathan has been attending Heather Brook nursery for six months. He started coming for two mornings a week at age two and a half. Staff at the nursery are all local and already knew Sara and her younger sister Shirelle 'from around and about'.

Nathan was enrolled at the nursery by Sara's probation officer. (Sara had been involved in a fight with her boyfriend – he had beaten her regularly – in which she fought back and assaulted him quite badly. He pressed charges and Sara received a community service order, which was why a probation officer was involved.)

Generally, Nathan is doing well at the nursery. He is happy and bright, always full of questions and eager to be involved in any activity. He particularly likes painting and would spend all day doing it if he could. According to staff 'he goes off into his own little world and will put layer after layer of paint on to the same piece of paper'.

Sara isn't a good timekeeper, so Nathan is sometimes late arriving and being picked up. He sometimes seems very tired and has to be left to sleep for the whole session. Sara says she has trouble waking him up in the mornings, but she feels he goes to bed at the appropriate time.

Sometimes other people collect Nathan, but Sara calls if it is going to be someone the nursery doesn't know. The nursery knows Nathan's grandmother, Joyce, as well as his aunt Shirelle. Joyce occasionally smells a bit of alcohol, but she is pleasant and known in the neighbourhood simply as 'enjoying a bit of a tipple'. Nathan is always pleased to see her and doesn't seem to play up when she arrives.

► Are there any issues of concern here?
► Are there any positive factors?
► Would you take any action at this point?
► Would you monitor the situation?
► Would you involve staff, Sara or Joyce? If so, how?
► Would you speak to the probation officer or other professionals, *eg* health visitor? If so, what would you say?

Over the next few weeks you become concerned as you notice the following:
► Nathan is arriving later and is collected more often by Sara's friends.
► He is more tired and appears lethargic and uninterested in activities.
► He is often hungry and seems more nervous of staff when they reprimand him or other children.

Look again at the six questions above. How would you respond to each of them now? Are your responses affected by the 'Notes to aid discussion' on page 30?

- Sara had been involved in a fight with her boyfriend. A wide range of research has found that witnessing violence to their mothers can have a detrimental impact on children that is equal to emotional abuse or psychological maltreatment (Kolbo, Blakely & Engleman 1996).
- Violence from partners to women may leave them with severe and permanent physical damage and can adversely affect their mental health. Apart from physical harm many women also experience loss of self-respect, low self-worth, feelings of hopelessness, depression and loss of confidence.
- Nathan goes 'off into his own little world' and is sometimes very tired. The age of the child witnessing domestic violence will influence how he interprets and manages his anxieties. Generally, pre-school children are more likely to have physical symptoms of their anxiety, such as stomach aches, bedwetting, sleeping difficulties, diarrhoea and asthma (Hester, Pearson & Harwin 1998; 2000).
- Nathan attends the nursery two mornings a week. Regular attendance provides a child with consistency, an opportunity to learn, to build positive relationships and develop a sense of self. It also demonstrates a commitment of care by parents.
- Nathan is doing well at the nursery. Successful social and emotional functioning in a day care setting is a positive demonstration of the child's development.
- Sara feels Nathan goes to bed at the appropriate time – she has some understanding that young children need boundaries, routines and plenty of sleep.
- Sara calls if Nathan is to be picked up by someone the nursery doesn't know – a sign of responsible parenting that recognises possible risks.
- Nathan's aunt and grandmother are known at the nursery. Knowing the family enables consistency for the child in terms of care and attachment.
- Nathan is always pleased to see Joyce. The reaction of a child to his carer can reflect their levels of confidence and trust in that relationship.

Nursery management is informed

Nathan's key person informs the nursery manager of her concerns. The manager considers all the information and looks at the form filled in by Sara when Nathan was registered at the nursery. She decides to call the referring probation officer and is told that:

- Sara has a history of alcohol abuse and is attending Alcoholics Anonymous as a condition of her probation order.
- Joyce has a chronic history of alcohol abuse and Sara says that she experienced regular physical chastisement as a child.
- Sara's ex-boyfriend was released from prison five weeks ago and is living in a probation hostel. He is known to be violent, and to abuse alcohol and drugs.

(Although this kind of information would usually be kept confidential under the Data Protection Act, child protection concerns take precedence.)

- What are the issues of concern here?
- Should the nursery manager take further action?
- Should the probation officer take further action?

[See Chapters 7 and 8 for guidance on working with colleagues and social services.]

Social services are informed

A few days later the probation officer calls the nursery manager to say that he will be visiting Sara in two days' time. They agree that he will talk to Sara about the concerns and explore how she is managing. But next day, no one turns up to collect Nathan. He had been brought in by a man not known to practitioners, and is particularly tired all day. The nursery manager calls Shirelle, who comes to collect Nathan.

When the probation officer visits Sara the following day, there is no answer at the door and he doesn't manage to see either Sara or Nathan. Both he and the nursery manager write to Sara asking her to contact them.

A week goes by and Nathan doesn't come to the nursery. The nursery manager calls the probation officer, who says that he has not seen Sara either. The nursery manager then calls social services and explains the situation, and her concerns. They already have child-protection concerns about Sara's ex-boyfriend.

Following the call, a social worker undertakes a core assessment and makes inquiries, coordinating all the information:

- Sara's alcohol use has increased. She has been using alcohol since she was 12 but has attended AA and really wants to stop drinking – she knows what growing up with an alcoholic mum is like. But she usually has Nathan with her when she goes to counselling, so can't always focus on or explore the issues in real depth.

- She is a binge drinker and drinks with several alcoholic friends.
- The ex-boyfriend has been trying to move back in, so Sara is staying out late at her friends' houses, drinking, in order to avoid him. Nathan falls asleep wherever they are and is woken to return home in the middle of the night.
- On other occasions Sara has left Nathan locked in his room, especially when there is violence.
- The ex-boyfriend has hit Nathan before.
- Sara is scared of her ex-boyfriend.
- Sara can't read very well and generally ignores letters.
- Sara has a 19-year-old brother, Robert, who is profoundly disabled. Joyce is his main carer when he is not at a residential school. Robert has returned home for Easter so Joyce is looking after him.
- As the 'big sister', Sara protected and cared for Shirelle and Robert when they were younger and, while pleased that Shirelle is at college and has her own flat, she feels resentful too.
- Sara is proud and won't ask her family to help unless she is too drunk to collect Nathan.

Agencies work together with the family

Social services hold a child protection conference. A coordinated protection plan for Nathan is drawn up and includes:

- increased nursery provision so that Nathan can attend every morning
- support for Sara with caring for Nathan, play and setting appropriate routines
- coordinated AA counselling and probation appointments for Sara when Nathan is in nursery
- GP-prescribed medication to assist with depression and the effects of alcohol withdrawal
- legal advice and assistance to help Sara keep her ex-boyfriend away
- provision by adult social services of home care for Robert when he is not at school
- help for Sara in finding and enrolling on an adult literacy course
- continuing assessment by a social worker with the potential to reconvene the conference if the situation deteriorates.

Sara says that she feels supported by this process even though she had been anxious about accepting social services' help in the fear that they would remove Nathan if all the circumstances came to light.

Not all children who witness domestic violence or live with parents who abuse alcohol or drugs or have mental health problems will be assessed as being at risk of, or experiencing, significant harm. However, children are most vulnerable when there is a cluster of these and it is often only when an investigation or assessment has started that the real extent of the problems is revealed. [See 'Mental illness, substance abuse and domestic violence', p. 15.]

The nursery's role leading up to the case conference

The nursery provided social services with key background information into the positive factors about Nathan and Sara's relationship, and the community context in which Nathan lives.

Initially, Sara was angry at social services being called in. She said the nursery was 'out of order' and 'had no right to tell anyone about her private business'. In response, the social worker explained to Sara the nursery's responsibilities in reporting concerns about children and told her that, once they had reported their concerns, the nursery also provided the social worker with positive comments. Sara was pleased that, among all the difficulties she had been having, Nathan was still happy at nursery and had been seen as 'happy and bright'.

The social worker arranged a meeting at Sara's house between Sara and Nathan's social services keyworker (the person appointed to work with Sara and help her through the current crisis – not to be confused with a day nursery's key person). This gave Sara a chance to 'say her piece'. The keyworker reassured her that only a few people knew all her personal details, that no one was thinking badly of her and that everyone would like to support her and Nathan. Sara realised that the nursery hadn't just jumped to conclusions, that they had worked with the probation officer in trying to find a way forward and to help her manage her difficulties.

The nursery manager and Nathan's keyworker attended the child protection conference and gave Sara a lift to the offices. The nursery looked after Nathan while the conference took place. Having the nursery staff at the conference gave Sara more confidence because they were familiar faces in a scary situation and because everything they said was true. [For details of what happens in a case conference, see 'Case conference', pp. 43–5.]

After the case conference

Sara didn't want to attend parenting groups; she was embarrassed. Instead, the keyworker discussed with Sara how she saw herself, how she saw Nathan and how she could best learn about parenting and managing Nathan's behaviour. Sara was able to consider the impact that alcohol abuse and stress had on Nathan's routines by reflecting on her own childhood experiences.

Sara and the keyworker devised a weekly programme of sessions that combined play sessions with Nathan. She and her keyworker also met with the nursery manager to discuss confidentiality and how the nursery would always try to speak to Sara first if they had concerns about Nathan. The nursery agreed that they would take time to talk through any letters or written notices that parents had to know about. Gradually, Sara was introduced to the weekly parent-support group which looks at lots of different aspects of parenting.

A 'core group' – a smaller meeting of some of the professionals involved in a case conference – reviews every protection plan. Nathan's keyworker was a member of his 'core group', which met at regular periods to review Nathan's protection plan and monitor progress. The keyworker reported that, while not everything was 'perfect', there were positive changes and Sara was committed to making improvements. This led the core group to recommend deregistration. After six months Nathan's name was taken off the child protection register at a review conference. The nursery support and other agency involvement continued. There were a few 'blips' (including a few very drunken binges), but Sara, her family, the GP, Alcoholics Anonymous and Nathan's nursery were all able to work together to make sure that Nathan was kept safe and not at risk of significant harm.

[For more about core groups, see 'Child protection plan', pp. 44–5.]

1 What should you do if you suspect abuse?

Your role in preventing or addressing the abuse of a child in your care starts with concern that the child may be at risk of harm. This concern might come to your attention in one of the following ways:

- your observations lead you to be concerned that you have identified signs of abuse [see Chapter 4]
- a child tells you about abuse they have experienced
- a third party, perhaps another child, shares their concerns with you.

Observation of an actual injury means that you need to consider immediate medical attention and immediate action to protect the child. In these circumstances it may be necessary for a practitioner to make immediate contact with the police and/or social services, or emergency health services. To do so, you will need to follow your setting's procedures for such contact [see Chapter 11].

A child who tells you they are being, or have been, abused has placed you in a position of trust: trust that you will act to help them, even if they ask you not to do anything or tell anyone. Don't underestimate the impact on you of hearing about abuse or identifying signs that a child might be at risk. Ensure that you know where to get support and who you can talk to.

Case study

Thomas, aged four and a half, is playing in the sand tray. His key person, Sally, sees that he has become absorbed while playing with two dolls: one male, the other female. Thomas is playing 'make believe' and the dolls are arguing. Sally hears the male doll telling the female doll to 'piss off'. Thomas then begins to hit the female doll violently with the male doll. The female doll is hit again and again until she is under the sand. Thomas throws the male doll on to the floor. Sally says to Thomas 'What did you do that for?' Thomas says, 'I hate Daddy. Daddy hits my mum. She cries. I hate him. He hurt me too.'

1 Jot down what you would say.
2 Jot down what you would *not* say.
3 Check against the following.

In this or a similar case, you should:
- react calmly so as not to frighten the child – find ways of comforting him
- take part in the child's play, though not if it is violent
- take him to a quiet area, if appropriate
- tell him he is right to tell
- tell him he is not to blame
- take what the child says seriously, while also recognising that he might not be playing out a precise replica of real life
- use words, phrases and signs that the child has used or understands, in keeping with his stage of development and method of communication – if necessary, ask someone else to assist with using his method of communication
- keep your questions to an absolute minimum – only ask questions that will help you understand what the child has chosen to tell you; don't ask about explicit details and don't ask leading questions
- reassure the child that the information will be kept private but that you have to tell certain people to make sure action is taken, and also that it is part of your job to make sure he is

kept safe (though be aware that, by telling the child that you have to tell *someone*, you may break the child's trust in you; they may not want anyone told)

▶ make a full record of what is being said, heard and seen, as soon as possible

▶ do not delay in passing the information on to the person in your setting who is responsible for child protection.

As an early years practitioner you already have the skills to communicate with young children. With issues of child protection many of these skills are vital in managing the situation. Try not to panic, and react as you might if there was another critical situation (see Think! box below).

Recording your concern

The impact of abuse on individual children is varied, so their responses will be varied too. Young children who are being abused may not appreciate or understand the gravity of what has happened to them so may not appear distressed or upset. This does not mean that they are OK, that the abuse has not affected them or that you should do nothing; it is important that all concerns are recorded, whether or not social services are involved.

When recording concern about a child's safety, the following should be written in ink:

▶ name and address of the child

Consider the scenario again, and the following responses made by Sally.

Thomas starts to cry. Sally sinks to her haunches and tries to hug Thomas, but he pulls away. Sally stands up. She asks Thomas, 'Does Daddy hit you around the head?' Thomas does not respond. He has stopped crying and is staring at the sand tray. Sally tries again. 'Would you like to tell me about it?' Thomas does not respond. 'You can tell me anything, you know.' Thomas still does not respond. Sally sighs and looks around for inspiration.

Sally does not achieve what she had hoped – she doesn't get more information from Thomas, and he has closed down on her.

▶ What are the key places where she took a wrong turn?

▶ What else could she have done that might have encouraged Thomas to tell her more?

In the end, Sally manages to move forward with Thomas. This is what happens:

'I tell you what,' says Sally. 'Why don't you come and help me put the painting things out? We're going to make splatty pictures with toothbrushes this afternoon, but some of the toothbrushes are too old to use. I could do with some help to work out which ones need to be thrown away.' Thomas says nothing. 'Come on,' Sally says. 'Doing something else might help us feel better.'

Thomas agrees to go with Sally. In the course of taking him back inside, chatting with him

while they get the toothbrushes and paints, Sally manages to bring Thomas back out of his shell. It also gives her a breathing space, time to regain her confidence and to think how else she might approach the situation. Sally and Thomas start playing a game with the toothbrushes as they sort through them. 'This one's to keep,' they say in a sing-song voice that goes up at the end. 'This one's to throw in the bin,' they say in a deep voice before throwing the toothbrush out. Thomas relaxes, and Sally feels confident that, while she hasn't got to the bottom of his earlier game, the crisis has passed.

As the sorting game develops, Sally and Thomas start competing with each other to see who can come up with a new way to describe the toothbrushes' condition: 'This one's a bright sunny day to keep', 'this one's a smelly sock to throw in the bin'; 'this one's a red rose to keep', 'this one's a dog poo to throw in the bin'. And so on until, at a point where they seem to have forgotten themselves and are giggling away, Thomas picks up an old toothbrush and says excitedly, 'This one's my daddy to throw in the bin.'

'Oh dear,' says Sally, who is suddenly shocked back into the earlier difficulty. 'Are you sure you want to put your daddy in the bin?'

'I do today,' Thomas shouts (he is still high from the game). 'Daddy hit Mummy in the tummy. He pushed me over too and I hit the wall.'

Jot down ideas about where Sally could take the conversation now. What else could she have done if Thomas had not opened up to her?

- age of the child, date of birth, ethnicity, religion or any disability
- name and address of significant adults
- date and time of the alleged incident
- nature of injury, or behaviour
- whether the child arrived at the setting with an injury
- child's explanation of what happened, in her own words
- adult's explanation of what happened
- any questions that were asked of the child
- date and time of the record
- signature of the person recording the incident.

Do not become overly concerned if any of the above information is not available to you. Do not pursue the questioning of the child for this information if it is not given freely. Consult any files or documentation you may have on the family for these details.

Records pertaining to issues of child protection may be accessible to social services, the police, the courts and solicitors, and may be presented to court. It is therefore important that you do not write speculative comments. Stick to the facts. Your opinion may be crucial, but ensure that it is *recorded* as an opinion and that you have evidence to support your view.

It is recommended that details of a child protection incident or concern should be recorded on a specific form. These should then be kept in line with your policies on record-keeping, record monitoring and file storage. There is a sample 'Record of concern' on pages 38–9, which you can photocopy and use.

Who do you tell? How do you tell?

Understanding signs and encouraging communication at the right level is not just something you need to do with children. There may also be barriers that halt effective communication between adults. These might include:
- timing – reporting a concern when someone is finishing her shift may mean she is not concentrating
- venue – you might not want to report a concern if other people are around
- power differences between practitioners, *eg* a new nursery nurse has concerns but is uncomfortable about approaching her manager
- assumptions about other professionals, *eg* social workers being interfering busybodies
- previous attempts to report concerns have not been taken seriously

- being distressed and unable to be clear about the information
- different languages and communication methods.

Good procedures will help avoid these problems and direct the actions of practitioners [see Chapter 11].

think

Imagine you are in the workplace and four-year-old Isabelle has a bruised eye and cheek. When asked, Isabelle says 'Daddy did it'. Write down answers to the following:
- Who will you tell?
- When you will tell them?
- If they are not available, who else needs to know?

You will probably have written down names of people you expect will take the matter forward. However, for the purposes of this exercise, imagine that the person you tell says 'I'm busy right now, and in any case Isabelle's always making up stories about home. Don't worry about it.' What would you do next? (The sections immediately below offer some guidance.)

Getting over barriers to professional communication

You have reported a concern but either nobody does anything or you think more should have been done. What do you do now?
Discuss your concerns with the person to whom you made the initial report (it may be one of your colleagues or someone based in social services). Think carefully about what it is you are unhappy about and, if you can, write it down before you have this discussion.

Child protection can be very emotive and sometimes having notes can help to keep things clear. Identify someone who is familiar with child protection and who can offer you some guidance – this might be a colleague or an independent adviser, *eg* from the NSPCC Helpline. Be persistent in getting your concerns listened to, but recognise that you may not be given all information if there is an ongoing police investigation or other need for confidentiality.

What if you are concerned that someone at your place of work is harming children?
The same principles apply. The difference is that the consequences for you, your colleague and your place of work are likely to be complicated and even more emotionally charged. The reporting process for this should be in your setting's child protection

procedures, though particular sensitivity is needed regarding:

▶ who you tell
▶ who you can get support from
▶ management decisions about the action to take within disciplinary procedures (*eg* should the member of staff be suspended while the investigation is carried out).

What if your concern is about a manager or someone else in a position of seniority?
If your concern relates to a senior manager or the person to whom you would normally report concerns, you will need to go to someone higher. If there isn't anyone, you should report your concern directly to social services, the police or the NSPCC. (There is a useful guide to drawing up a whistleblowing policy produced by Public Concern at Work (2001), though do note that it is aimed at organisations with more than 20 members of staff, and costs £300 to buy).

Are you worried that you might lose your job if you make a fuss?
The anxiety and fear that surround reporting any abuse or concern can be great, especially if you are blowing the whistle on someone in a position of power in your organisation. But if you decide to keep quiet, who will act to protect the child(ren) you are worried about? In the past, staff have gone to extreme lengths in order to be heard, including cases where workers in residential homes have written to the government and newspapers when the local authority failed to listen to them. This takes a lot of energy, commitment and perseverance. You will need to balance this with the distress, devastation and guilt you may feel if you do nothing and the child(ren) continue to be harmed. A better understanding about child protection will help you feel more confident when weighing up all these complicated issues.

Response to suspected child abuse: a reference map

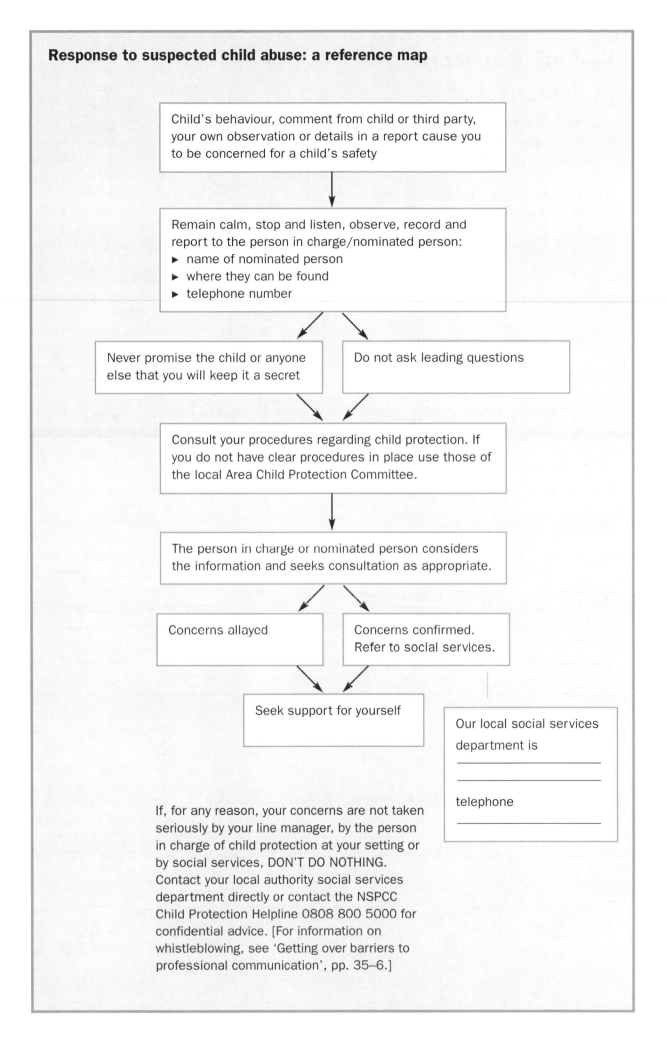

Child's behaviour, comment from child or third party, your own observation or details in a report cause you to be concerned for a child's safety

Remain calm, stop and listen, observe, record and report to the person in charge/nominated person:
► name of nominated person
► where they can be found
► telephone number

Never promise the child or anyone else that you will keep it a secret

Do not ask leading questions

Consult your procedures regarding child protection. If you do not have clear procedures in place use those of the local Area Child Protection Committee.

The person in charge or nominated person considers the information and seeks consultation as appropriate.

Concerns allayed

Concerns confirmed. Refer to social services.

Seek support for yourself

Our local social services department is

_____

_____

telephone

_____

If, for any reason, your concerns are not taken seriously by your line manager, by the person in charge of child protection at your setting or by social services, DON'T DO NOTHING. Contact your local authority social services department directly or contact the NSPCC Child Protection Helpline 0808 800 5000 for confidential advice. [For information on whistleblowing, see 'Getting over barriers to professional communication', pp. 35–6.]

Record of concern

CONFIDENTIAL

Use continuation sheets as necessary.
Complete in black ink.

Date and time of this record _____

Name and address of the child _____

_____

Age and date of birth _____

Ethnicity _____

Religion/faith _____

Name, address and phone number of person/s with parental responsibility

1 _____

2 _____

3 _____

Legal status of child (if looked after) _____

The organisation's role with the child _____

What is the child's communication method? Please describe.

_____

Does the child have specific mobility/health needs?

_____

Date and time of the alleged incident _____

Name and address of adults or other children/young people involved

1 _____

2 _____

3 _____

4 _____

5 _____

Nature of injury, behaviour or concern

_____

_____

Observations made by you or reported to you (*eg* description of visible bruising or injury, child's emotional state)

_____

_____

When and how did the concern first come to your notice?

_____

Has the child been spoken to? If so by whom and what was said?

_____

_____

Give the child's explanation of what happened in his/her own words/means of communication

_____

_____

_____

Does anyone else have an explanation of what happened?
If so who are they and what did they say?

_____

Have the parents/carers been contacted? If so what was said?

_____

_____

Have there been any previous concerns? If so, what are they? Give details and locate any record of these.

_____

_____

Any relevant background information _____

_____

Has anybody else been consulted, any other action been taken or any other questions asked? If so, provide details.

_____

Signature _____

Name of person recording the incident _____

Position of person recording the incident _____

8 Child protection investigation process

Local authority social services departments must investigate all reports of suspected child abuse [see Appendix 1]. They have a duty to 'safeguard and promote the welfare of children in their area who are in need' (Children Act 1989), including children in need of protection, and must ensure that there is an Area Child Protection Committee (ACPC) covering their area. The ACPC is a multi-agency forum for agreeing how the different services and professional groups should work together to safeguard children in that area, and for making sure that arrangements work effectively to bring about good outcomes for children (contact details for local ACPCs are available at www.doh.gov.uk/acpc).

Social services departments have different structures but there is generally a social work team responsible for receiving and following up reports or referrals about children. The government has published guidance on the process for investigation (Department of Health *et al.* 1999) and for services which assess, protect or support children in need (Department of Health *et al.* 2000). The number of your local social services department will be listed in the telephone directory under the name of the local authority. You may already be in contact with a social worker or under-eights coordinator (either in social services or the local education authority) who has visited your setting or is responsible for your funding arrangements. Do make use of any such existing contacts for advice or guidance.

During a child protection investigation, social services, the police or the NSPCC will gather all relevant information about the child and the circumstances of the concern. All child protection investigations are undertaken jointly between the police and social services. The extent of police involvement may vary, depending on the nature of the case. The police become involved because a criminal offence may have taken place if a child has been abused, and also because they have greater emergency legal powers to protect children. Police authorities have specially trained officers in units or teams to undertake child protection investigations. These will have different names or titles in different parts of the country, and might be the Child and Family Support Unit, or the Child Protection Unit.

There has been a lot in the news about social workers not responding properly to reports of suspected abuse due to overwork. Don't let that put you off; if social workers don't respond to a reported concern, keep going, keep reporting it.

Planning the investigation

Whenever there is reasonable cause to suspect that a child is suffering or is likely to suffer significant harm, there should be a strategy discussion involving social services, the police, other appropriate agencies (*eg* education or health) and any referring agency (which might be a nursery or Sure Start programme). This discussion is usually organised and managed by social services. Refer to your local ACPC for confirmation.

The purpose of a strategy discussion is to plan inquiries. The discussion may take place at the point of referral or at any other time during the course of inquiries, as necessary. It may take the form of a meeting at social services offices, the police station or another convenient location such as a referring early years setting. Meetings are crucial if a case is particularly complicated, but in some cases telephone discussions may be sufficient – or even essential if a child is at such risk that quick action is required to ensure protection.

Discussions will involve the following individuals:
▶ social worker assigned to the case
▶ police officer assigned to the case
▶ the person making the referral, where possible
▶ the child's key person, class teacher or other appropriate member of setting/school staff.

Other people who may be included in a strategy discussion include:
▶ a specialist adviser (*eg* translator or signer)
▶ GP
▶ health visitor
▶ school nurse
▶ legal adviser.

The strategy discussion is between professionals, and is not likely to involve the parents or children at this stage. If the concerns are about more than one child, professionals representing each child will be involved.

In the course of a strategy discussion the available information will be shared, reviewed and clarified, and participants will aim to identify or agree on:

▶ whether to initiate Section 47 inquiries or continue them if they have already begun (the term 'Section 47 inquiries' is another name for a child protection investigation; it refers to Section 47 of the Children Act 1989 [see Appendix 1, p. 62])
▶ when the child and family will be interviewed, for what purposes and by whom
▶ how the child will be interviewed, *ie* video-recorded or not, and by whom
▶ where the interviews will take place
▶ whether the available information suggests that the child should have a medical examination and, if so, who is to carry it out (if no medical examination is to take place, the reasons should be recorded)
▶ any action that is needed immediately to safeguard the child
▶ the provision of interim services and support for the child
▶ a person with parental responsibility who may give consent, *eg* for an interview with or medical examination of the child
▶ what information about the strategy discussion is to be shared with the family
▶ any specialist assistance which may be needed (*eg* an interpreter for families with English as an additional language)
▶ an appropriate person to support the child during the inquiry process, if this is not to be a parent or other family member
▶ a plan for Section 47 inquiries as part of the core assessment
▶ contingency plans (*eg* whether the child needs to be removed from the family home)
▶ the needs of any other children who may be affected (*eg* siblings and other children in contact with alleged abusers).

Where the child is disabled, with physical impairments or learning difficulties, the strategy discussion/meeting must:

▶ make no assumptions that a disabled child is unable to be interviewed or give credible evidence
▶ carry out a full assessment of the child's abilities and needs, *eg* access to buildings if the child uses a wheelchair.

In all cases, the age and ability of the child must be taken into consideration.

The role of an early years practitioner in a strategy discussion

think

Jot down how you think you might be involved in the following:
▶ a meeting at the social services offices
▶ a telephone discussion with a social worker.
Given the purpose of strategy discussions, what kind of information might you need to share?

Investigation and assessment

The child's parents are contacted as soon as an investigation begins. They are asked to assist social services with their inquiries and are kept informed about what is happening. The only time parents do not know that inquiries are under way is if there is reason to believe that telling them would endanger the child's safety. In this situation, the social worker and/or police can obtain a court order allowing them to take action to protect the child – except in an extreme emergency, where the police have legal powers to do so.

At this point, everyone who is relevant to the investigation is interviewed. This includes parents, family members, other adults in the house, colleagues if the suspected abuse occurred at work, and the person who reported the concern. A child is interviewed if he is judged to be old enough and at an appropriate stage of development – and every attempt is made to portray his experiences and views accurately, and to abide by his wishes and feelings.

Other agencies and individuals, such as health visitors, GPs, nursery staff or teachers (if they were not present at the strategy discussion) will be asked what they know about the child, whether they have ever had reason to be concerned or if they have any other information that may assist the investigation. An early years practitioner involved in this part of the process is most likely to be interviewed at her place of work by a social worker and/or police officer. If the practitioner has information which might be needed as evidence in a criminal prosecution, the police may request a witness statement. This statement may be taken at the setting, the police station or at the practitioner's home, depending on the circumstances of the case.

An early years practitioner may be called upon to accompany a child or family member during the inquiries. In this case, the social worker and police officer will maintain the lead responsibility, but you should be

Child protection investigation process: a reference map

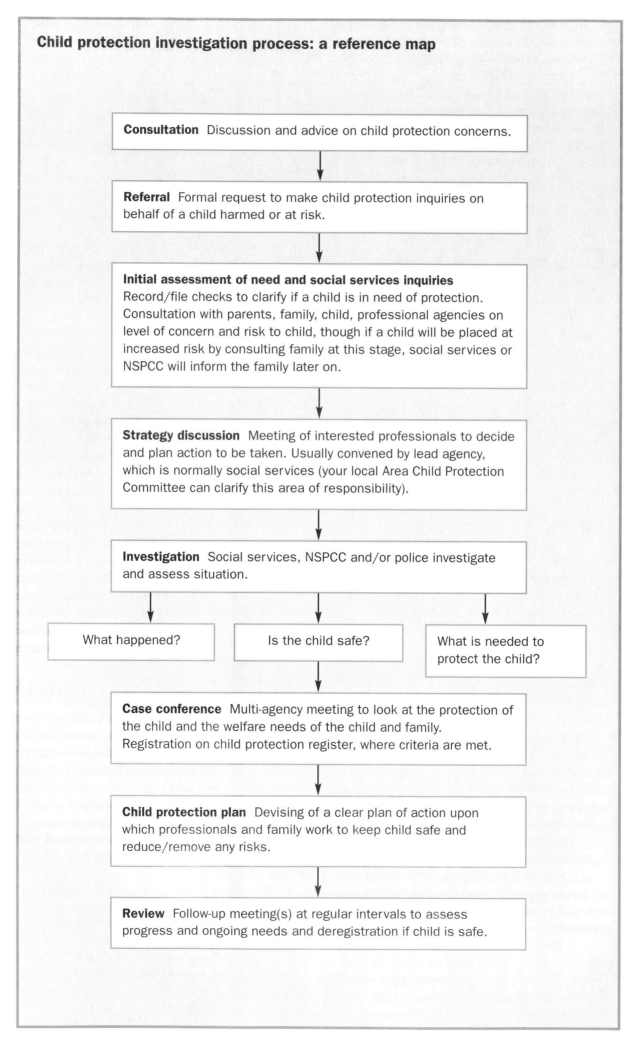

Consultation Discussion and advice on child protection concerns.

↓

Referral Formal request to make child protection inquiries on behalf of a child harmed or at risk.

↓

Initial assessment of need and social services inquiries
Record/file checks to clarify if a child is in need of protection. Consultation with parents, family, child, professional agencies on level of concern and risk to child, though if a child will be placed at increased risk by consulting family at this stage, social services or NSPCC will inform the family later on.

↓

Strategy discussion Meeting of interested professionals to decide and plan action to be taken. Usually convened by lead agency, which is normally social services (your local Area Child Protection Committee can clarify this area of responsibility).

↓

Investigation Social services, NSPCC and/or police investigate and assess situation.

↓   ↓   ↓

| What happened? | Is the child safe? | What is needed to protect the child? |

↓

Case conference Multi-agency meeting to look at the protection of the child and the welfare needs of the child and family. Registration on child protection register, where criteria are met.

↓

Child protection plan Devising of a clear plan of action upon which professionals and family work to keep child safe and reduce/remove any risks.

↓

Review Follow-up meeting(s) at regular intervals to assess progress and ongoing needs and deregistration if child is safe.

available to discuss your role. It is OK to ask questions about what is happening and why, though you may not always receive a detailed answer – because of time constraints or confidentiality, or because there is no answer to your question at that time. Social workers and police undertaking child protection investigations have training and experience that give them skill and sensitivity in managing investigations. But your knowledge of the child and family, and your skills and experience of working with children could be invaluable in assisting the investigation. Your involvement and cooperation will help to ensure that the investigation has the best outcome for the child and family.

If the child is believed to have physical injuries or to show evidence of a sexual assault, she is likely to be medically examined. This is undertaken by a doctor: either a GP or paediatrician who has had training in child protection. Social services or the police are responsible for arranging this. Unless a court order has been obtained, someone with parental responsibility must give permission for a medical examination.

A parent or carer remains with the child throughout the investigation, as long as this does not jeopardise it. If a parent is suspected or considered not to act in the best interests of the child then another family member or significant person will support the child (this person will have been identified in the strategy discussion). An early years practitioner may have contact with the family or child around this time and could be valuable in offering support and reassurance, explaining processes and ensuring that the child's best interests always remain a focus for the family.

According to the *Framework for the assessment of children in need and their families* (Department of Health *et al.* 2000), initial assessments must be undertaken within seven working days of the date of referral, and a core assessment within a further 35 working days. It may be that the outcome of the investigation finds that the child is not in need of protection. However, if child protection concerns are confirmed there may be a case conference.

Case conference

The purpose of a case conference is to:
▶ bring together all the information that has been gathered about the child's health, development and wellbeing

▶ present information about the parents' capacity to ensure the child's safety and promote the child's welfare
▶ make judgements about the likelihood of a child suffering significant harm in the future
▶ decide what future action is needed to safeguard the child and promote her welfare, how that action will be taken forward, and with what intended outcomes.

Formal decisions about whether a person has harmed a child (a criminal offence) are not made at this conference, as issues of 'guilt' or 'culpability' are investigated by the police and decided by the courts. Nor is the conference a forum in which to air grievances or complaints about agency actions or between parents. There are other processes for this.

Who attends a case conference?

A case conference brings together all the professionals most involved with the child and family [see list below]. Depending on local procedures, the child's parents, where appropriate, will also be invited to take part, and perhaps some other family members. Young children are unlikely to be invited to attend, but the social worker who has spoken to the child will present their views, wishes and feelings. Older children may be given the option to attend all or part of the conference.

Individuals attending the case conference will speak from professional experience, knowledge of the child or family, or both. This is an inter-agency meeting, and a minimum number of agencies must be present for a conference to take place. This minimum is generally representatives from three of the following:
▶ social services
▶ health services (GP, health visitor, midwife, community nurse, school nurse)
▶ education services (teacher, nursery nurse, education social worker)
▶ police
▶ voluntary agencies (*eg* Home-Start)
▶ housing authority
▶ probation officer
▶ court welfare officer.

Professionals and agencies that are invited but are unable to attend should provide a written report which can be read out in conference – and as an early years practitioner you might well end up doing this. If so, social services can give you guidance about what to write; it is usually a summary of what you know about the child, the family background and the child protection concerns.

There is often more than one representative from an agency (eg a nursery manager may accompany the child's key person to a conference), and social services are likely to have various people in attendance, depending upon the case. They might include:

► investigating social worker and manager
► child care team social worker
► looked-after services social worker
► foster carer(s).

Other people attending might include:

► religious leaders or other community support
► interpreters
► solicitors
► guardian ad litem (an individual who can speak for the child and act in her interests should the child be subject to court proceedings).

There might be a solicitor for the local authority and a solicitor for the family. Solicitors can only give advice and guidance to the person they represent; they do not have a role in giving an opinion on the case or contributing to the decisions of the case conference.

The family may want a supporter to attend with them – a friend, neighbour or family member.

If a professional or a family member is concerned about violence or intimidation from another family member, the conference chair may exclude that person. The chair can also exclude anyone who disrupts or tries to sabotage the meeting by, for example, shouting, being abusive or interrupting.

Some people may feel worried about speaking in a meeting like this and in front of people they have never met. The conference chair should help by introducing everyone, explaining why they are there, and offering reassurance. Emotions can run high in case conferences: parents may cry, shout or be angry; professionals may give information that is inaccurate, may disagree, talk over or contradict a parent. The chair should manage this sensitively but firmly, ensuring that the reason for the meeting – to consider the child's safety – remains its focus.

If you attend a case conference you might take some time to:

► think about what you know, and how you are going to say it
► decide what is fact and what is your opinion

► make some notes or prepare a report to take with you
► talk to your manager or supervisor, and ask if she will come with you
► talk to the family about your role at the conference
► arrange cover at work
► find out how to get to the conference venue.

If you are called to a case conference, guidelines and information should be made available to you on how the meeting will be run. These guidelines are available from social services and should describe the conference process in your area. The Family Rights Group can also offer assistance [see Appendix 2 for details].

What is decided in a case conference?

The concern of all the professionals involved is to ensure the safety and wellbeing of the child, and the investigation and case conference may result in a number of different outcomes.

Child's name placed on child protection register

In this case, a key worker (social worker) is appointed to coordinate the help that is given to the family concerned, and to be the contact person for information about the family and the child. If you attend a case conference in a professional role you will be asked for your view as to whether a child's name should be placed on the register. The chair will help all the conference members to make this important decision.

The child protection register is held confidentially in every local authority, and a child's name can only be placed on it if a case conference decides that she is at continuing risk of significant harm. If a child's details are placed on the register, all agencies have to provide whatever services are necessary to protect that child. This is written down in a child protection plan.

The only people who can find out which children are on the register are social services, the police and, in an emergency, health services. This means that if a child arrives in hospital with injuries that look suspicious, a doctor can check the register and alert the police and social services if the child's name appears on it.

Child protection plan

When a child's name is placed on the child protection register, the work that needs to be done, why, when and by whom is set out in a child protection plan which is decided upon at the case conference. The plan describes the identified needs of the child, and what must happen to keep the child safe and reduce any risk of abuse. The work might involve further assessment of the child and family to make sound judgements on how best to safeguard the child, and this may include a need for:

▶ medical treatment
▶ therapeutic services
▶ behaviour management
▶ anger management
▶ parenting skills
▶ family support (eg helping with parenting tasks in the home by a voluntary agency such as Home-Start)
▶ respite care
▶ day care
▶ domiciliary services
▶ psychological or psychiatric services
▶ education support.

Early years practitioners and their services might be able to take an active role in providing some of this support, and it is worth thinking about the kind of help you may be able to offer.

The child protection plan will identify a core group of people responsible for putting the protection plan into action, which must meet within ten working days of the case conference. The members of this group will include the social services keyworker, certain professionals (as at case conference), family members and the child, if appropriate. The keyworker will arrange the core group's meetings, which will be smaller and less formal than the case conference. The group has to make sure that:

▶ the actions in the child protection plan are happening
▶ the child is benefiting from those actions
▶ the child is being protected
▶ changes are made to the plan if necessary.

There will be a written record of the core group meetings.

An early years practitioner can sometimes be a member of this core group, and should always seek guidance and support from managers and colleagues during any such involvement. If you are called upon to be part of a core group, it may be useful to meet with the social worker separately to talk through what has happened, and discuss the child protection plan and your role in the process.

The aim of the child protection plan is to ensure that the child does not remain at risk of significant harm. Review case conferences are held after three months, then at six-monthly intervals. Once a child is deemed to be no longer at risk, the child's name is removed from the register and social services involvement may cease, unless there remains a need for some other services that they provide.

Court action

In serious cases, the case conference may recommend that court action be taken. The courts can decide whether a child should remain at home, under a Supervision Order, or be placed away from home for his own safety. If a child is removed from home, attempts will be made to change family circumstances so that the child can live with his own family in safety. No professional decides to remove a child from his family home unless she is fully convinced that this is in the best interests of the child.

It is possible that you will be called upon to be a witness in court proceedings. The information that you give to the court or share with other professionals should be clear and factual. Do not allow yourself to be swayed by more persuasive participants, or to be inhibited by the presence of parents or other professionals or by their involvement in the proceedings. A clear account, based on your observations, notes or records will avoid potential confusion and allow the court to reach an assessment of what is best for the child.

If you are called to be a witness, you may feel anxious about the event. Support should be available to you through your line manager, national organisation or local authority under-eights adviser (this contact will be particularly helpful for practitioners working alone, such as childminders or nannies). You should talk to the child's key worker, who will be familiar with the court process.

Court proceedings will only be taken in severe and extreme circumstances, and worries about the possibility of being involved in this should never deter you from sharing your worries about a child with another professional – in your setting, service, local EYDCP, local authority or professional association to which you belong or are affiliated (eg National Childminding Association, National Day Nurseries Association, Pre-school Learning Alliance).

After the case conference

Following the case conference and, possibly, a court decision, the child may remain at home, be with another family member or in full-time local authority care. You may have been involved in the child protection process or come across a child in your organisation who has been through this experience. This has probably been an upsetting and traumatic time for her. Your help and support at this time can make all the difference. You should continue to provide a warm and friendly environment for the child concerned, as you would for all children. Reassure her that you are available to help. This might be achieved by ensuring that:

▶ new carers are aware of the child's likes, dislikes and routines

▶ favourite toys and stories are kept with the child

▶ the child has extra time with and attention from her key person or class teacher

▶ appropriate staff are informed about the situation so that it can be taken into account when managing the child's behaviour

▶ play and activities provide the child with opportunities to express feelings in a safe environment.

On occasion, parents or older children may wish to complain about the process, outcome or decisions taken by a conference. Social services departments will have procedures to deal with complaints. Individual agencies may also wish to register a complaint, either about the process or in respect of the services provided (or not provided) as a result of assessments or the conference itself. These should be conveyed to the agency concerned and responded to in accordance with its own procedures for such matters.

No further action

A child protection investigation does not always result in a case conference. Sometimes concerns are not substantiated or there is not enough evidence for agencies to pursue the concerns. This can result in a decision to take no further action.

These situations can be problematic and may present difficulties for the family, early years practitioners and the investigating agency.

Unsubstantiated concerns
Once concerns have been reported, the purpose of the investigation is to determine whether a child is at risk of, or is experiencing, significant harm. The investigation process has been developed to try and find out as much information as possible, analyse it and reach an informed conclusion in order to protect children. By systematically asking questions, gathering information and looking at the evidence, social services, the police and the NSPCC (if they are involved) may find out that the concerns are not as they first seemed.

Families having to experience a child protection investigation where no cause for concern is found, are likely to feel angry at being put through an investigation and being 'falsely' accused. If it was you or your setting who reported a concern, the family may direct these feelings back towards you. In a different situation, you may feel angry that a family you know had to deal with an investigation when you 'knew' there was no cause for concern.

It is often hard to manage these feelings. Good practice adopted by social services, the police and the NSPCC (if involved) will hopefully ease them by explaining the reasons why an investigation occurred and by treating people with respect. The systems and processes have been developed after years of learning through practice, research and tragic experiences of children being left at risk of abuse.

You may be able to help families (and yourself) through these difficult times by helping them understand the process of a child protection investigation. Feeling out of control and powerless when faced with the 'big power' of the child protection system contributes to their distress, especially as most parents will have previously experienced absolute control over making decisions for their child. But even angry and distressed families often understand why an investigation has taken place if it is explained in a way they can understand. Parents are unlikely to enjoy the experience of being under investigation, but are often grateful that systems are in place to protect their child. Empowering parents by advising them of their right to complain, to have access to records or even to ask questions enables them to exercise some power and control.

Sometimes, while there may be no further cause for concern in terms of protection, a child might be identified as being in need. In such cases, social services are required to offer support such as a nursery place, childminding or referral to other agencies.

Insufficient evidence
An investigation may be unable to demonstrate a cause for concern. If you made

the report you may have to continue working with a child while believing that he has been or is being abused. There are many reasons why an investigation may not identify abuse. Assessing and identifying risk of significant harm is complex and can be affected by many factors including:

▶ there may be no observable physical evidence such as bruising or injury
▶ evidence, such as a stick used to hit or a rope used to tie up might be hidden or destroyed
▶ a plausible explanation may be given by a caregiver or the perpetrator
▶ there may be no witnesses other than the child
▶ the child may have been silenced – he may not say what happened or may give a false account
▶ other adults/children may lie about what they know through fear, intimidation, ignorance or collusion.

For an early years practitioner, the family and any professionals involved, this can raise significant issues of frustration, anger and fear. And imagine how it might feel for the child.

Sometimes it may take several investigations before the truth of a situation comes to light. Individuals may decide after the fourth incident, for example, that they will tell the truth or report all the concerns. Children have said:

▶ 'If only the social worker had asked my granddad. He knew what was happening.' But the social worker was not told the granddad even existed, let alone looked after the child.
▶ 'My mum lied and told the social worker I got bruised by falling down the stairs again. My childminder liked my mum. They were friends. So my childminder didn't tell the social worker about my mum getting drunk and beating me.'
▶ 'My older sister thought he wasn't doing it to me. We didn't want Dad to go to prison and us to go to care. So I said nothing. I watched the social worker walking away.'

These examples show that, when there is insufficient evidence to prove that a child is at risk, everyone involved must be vigilant and supportive, manage the situation sensitively and provide safe, responsible care. Maintaining positive relationships may empower someone to speak out, enable other evidence to be identified and, at the very least, contribute to the child's resilience in managing abuse if there is any.

There may also come a point when practitioners must face the fact that they misinterpreted a situation and that there is genuinely no cause for concern.

9 **How did Mo get hurt?** Case study 2

The initial situation

▶ Mo Reece, aged two and a half years (child)
▶ Carl Reece, aged 35 years (father)
▶ Aideen Reece, aged 30 years (mother)
▶ Joan Day, childminder
▶ Patrick Day, aged four years (childminder's son)

Mo has been attending Bangor Road Nursery in Belfast three afternoons a week since she was 18 months old. Mr and Mrs Reece both work, Carl as a computer programmer and Aideen as a university lecturer in nutrition. Joan, a family friend and childminder, has cared for Mo since she was six months old, when Aideen returned to work. Joan brings Mo to nursery and either Aideen or Carl collects her. Mo has always been regarded as a happy, contented child reaching all her developmental milestones. Until recently she has seemed balanced and secure in the care arrangements, and had no medical or particular needs.

But over the last six weeks Mo's key person, Holly, has noticed a marked change in her behaviour. To begin with Holly couldn't really describe the difference; Mo just didn't seem as happy. The changes grew more specific as Mo became quiet, more sleepy, more clingy and seeking cuddles, and once rocked herself with her hands holding her crotch.

Holly made a note of the changes and tried to speak to Carl about them. He said all was OK: Mo was sleeping normally at home and he hadn't any worries about her. Holly also asked Joan, who said Aideen had told her that Mo had had a few disturbed nights with a wet bed, but she wasn't worried and had discussed the behaviour in general terms of development and Mo's growing confidence with wearing no nappies.

There is also a significant change in Mo's response when Carl picks her up. She has begun to experience furious tantrums when he collects her, having been 'all dad' before (Aideen has often commented on how naturally fatherhood comes to Carl). When asked about the new behaviour, Carl says that he and Aideen are both having a busy time with work; that Aideen is publishing a paper written for the British Medical Association.

Holly has identified some changes in **think** Mo's behaviour and discussed them with both Carl and Joan, neither of whom have any concerns about Mo.
▶ What notes would you have made of these conversations?
▶ Is there anyone else Holly should speak to?
▶ What might Mo's behaviours indicate?
▶ Should the nursery take any further action at this point?

Two weeks pass and then, soon after arriving at nursery at the usual time (12.30) on a Friday, Mo wets herself and becomes very upset, sobbing inconsolably. Holly takes Mo to the toilet to change her clothes, reassure her and calm her down. While changing Mo, Holly sees bruising on Mo's vagina and inner thigh. Holly says to Mo 'What have you done here, Mo? Have you got a poorly?' Mo doesn't say anything but does calm down and, once changed, goes to play at the sandpit. Holly goes to tell Cassie, the nursery manager, about Mo's unusual bruises. (Cassie is also the designated person for child protection and has received training about safeguarding children so that she can undertake this role.)

Cassie and Holly discuss everything they know about Mo. Cassie asks Holly if she thinks the bruising could have been accidental. Holly says she doesn't know but that usually, if Mo has fallen over or anything, Joan tells staff when she drops her off. Cassie also asks if there have been any other concerns about Mo. Holly looks at her notes and tells Cassie about the behaviour changes over the previous eight weeks. Cassie is aware that all these factors might be indicators of abuse but that the nursery needs to find out more before jumping to conclusions.

▶ What abuse might the bruising **think** indicate?
▶ What abuse might the behavioural changes indicate?
▶ Do you think Mo is, or has been, at risk of significant harm?
▶ What should the nursery do now?
▶ Are there any other options?

The nursery takes action

Cassie and Holly agree on the following action:
1 Cassie will phone Joan immediately and say,

'We've noticed Mo has some bruises and, as you know, it's our policy to make sure injuries are accounted for. Do you know anything about them?' In their discussion, Cassie and Holly had acknowledged how important it is not to say anything which might jeopardise an investigation, so Cassie will not automatically say where the bruising is, as a perpetrator may have an opportunity to think of an explanation, or cover up for someone. And if Mo has experienced abuse no one knows who the abuser is, so caution is vital when speaking to anyone.

2 Holly will engage Mo and attempt to communicate with her about how she got the bruises, without asking leading questions.

3 Cassie will advise her senior officer that Holly may be engaged in an issue that has arisen with Mo and they may have to release her to spend all of her time with Mo for the rest of the day.

This is what happens when they put their strategy into play. Cassie phones Joan but there is no answer. She tries again after half an hour but there is still no answer. Holly attempts to engage Mo to find out about the bruises but Mo shrugs and says, 'Naughty owww!' Mo then has an afternoon sleep during quiet time.

Cassie and Holly are aware that time is passing: it is now 3.00 and Carl is due to collect Mo at 4.30. They try calling Joan again, but there is still no answer.

Cassie decides to telephone Carl at work but is told he is at an off-site meeting until 4.00, when he will leave to collect Mo. The office receptionist agrees to try and get a message to Carl that he should call the nursery, but his mobile is on answer machine. Cassie calls Aideen on her mobile, but it too goes straight to an answer machine.

Carl finally calls the nursery at 4.05 while driving to the nursery. When he is told that Mo has bruising he makes comments like, 'Well all kids get bumps' and 'It's nothing to worry about'. When Cassie suggests that they need to talk about it, Carl becomes suspicious and says, 'Oh great, that's all we need. Look, we're going away for the week-end with a doctor friend. I'll get him to sort her out.' And then, 'What have you done to her?'

When Carl arrives he is harassed and in a hurry. He says he doesn't know anything about any bruises, asks if Joan said anything and asks Cassie where the bruises are. Cassie says that they are on Mo's legs. Cassie attempts to explain to Carl why she is concerned and why she needs to be sure about Mo's safety. Carl becomes angry, saying, 'What are you accusing me of? If anything happened to my daughter I'll sue you. I'll kill anyone who hurts my daughter.' And, 'She's probably fallen over'.

With that he goes to the cloakroom, scoops up Mo and leaves the nursery.

think

▶ Should social services be called?
▶ Should the police be called?
▶ Write down what information you think is important about (a) describing the concern or suspicion (b) the family background.

Social services are informed

Cassie decides that she must consult social services immediately, and calls the duty team. The social worker takes all the details about the cause for concern, along with background information about Mo and the family. Social services decide to make inquiries under Section 47 of the Children Act 1989 [see Appendix 1, p. 62], to assess whether Mo is at risk of, or has experienced, significant harm. Social services agree to inform the nursery on Monday of the outcome of the investigation.

An experienced duty social worker, Josephine Bird, is allocated the case. The following telephone inquiries are made (she is able to make these inquiries, despite the restrictions on confidentiality imposed by the Data Protection Act 1998 because the concerns merit a Section 47 child protection investigation):

▶ social services records – the family's details do not appear
▶ child protection register – Mo's name is not on it
▶ GP – Mo has received regular services, has been given all her immunisations and reached all developmental milestones; the GP has no particular cause for concern but agrees that further inquiries should be made
▶ childminder, Joan Day – no answer
▶ police – they have no immediate knowledge of any family members but agree that it is necessary to make a joint visit to the family that evening.

These phone calls constitute the strategy discussion because it is felt that swift action is needed. The reasons for this are as follows:

▶ it is now 5.30pm and, as it is a Friday, no agencies (nursery, GP, etc) will see Mo until Monday
▶ if Mo is at risk of further harm she could be abused over the weekend
▶ the genital bruising and behavioural observations could indicate sexual abuse with physical assault

- Mo may have been physically assaulted and other injuries may be present elsewhere on her body
- Mo's age makes her more vulnerable to abuse and at greater risk of serious physical injury from assault
- if she has been abused the perpetrator may 'silence' her by threats
- bruising may be medical evidence of abuse; bruises fade over time.

At 6.30pm, Josephine Bird and a female police officer call at the Reece home. Initially, Carl is shocked and upset. Josephine and the police officer explain their roles and the legal framework for their inquiries. Josephine asks if they can go into another room to talk, away from Mo, who is watching a Bob the Builder video. They go into the kitchen.

Carl says he knows why they are there and is angry that the nursery has called them. However, he is also relieved because he has looked at Mo's legs and vagina and seen the bruising. He wants to get to the bottom of it because he has no idea how the bruises have happened, and if someone has hurt her he wants them 'done'. He asks if they think someone at the nursery might have hurt her.

During the interview, Josephine and the police officer ask about everyone who looks after Mo, when and where. They discover that Aideen has been going to England a lot over the past eight weeks while her book is being published, and this has meant some overnight stays – something which has never happened before and which has made Mo unhappy. Carl mentions that Mo's attitude towards him picking her up from nursery changed suddenly when Aideen started to stay away overnight. He guesses his appearance at the end of the day was taken by Mo as a clear sign that her Mummy wouldn't be at home – hence her fury at seeing him. Aideen was away earlier in the week, returning Thursday. She is currently at work and is due back any minute.

There is still no explanation for the bruising. However, the information about Aideen being away a lot constitutes a significant change in family circumstances and this may have influenced the changes in Mo's behaviour observed by the nursery – including her reluctance to be picked up by Carl.

Josephine and the police officer agree that the childminder, Joan, may have information about the bruising. Josephine phones Joan, who says that Mo did hurt herself the day before (Thursday) and that she told Aideen all about it. The accident happened when Mo climbed on Patrick's bicycle (Patrick is Joan's four-year-old son). Joan told Mo to get off because the bike is far too big for her, but at that moment Mo slipped and fell on to the crossbar, hitting herself quite hard between the legs. Mo cried and Joan comforted her. There was reddening to Mo's legs at the time and Joan says that, in her experience, this type of accident might cause bruising. Mo had gone to the toilet by herself that morning so Joan didn't see if any bruises had come out. When prompted, Joan says she knows she forgot to mention the fall to nursery that morning (Friday). It had happened the day before (Mo doesn't go to nursery on Thursday afternoons) and she was in a hurry to get Patrick to a doctor's appointment.

Joan reaffirms reports from the GP, saying that she has absolutely no concerns about the care Mo receives from her parents or from the nursery. Joan says she is happy for Josephine and the police officer to visit or speak to her again if necessary, and asks to be told of any outcome.

Aideen comes home just as Josephine concludes the phone call. She is incredibly shocked to find a social worker and police officer in her house and, panicked, thinks that something has happened to Mo. Once she has seen Mo and calmed down, Carl tells her what has happened: that Mo has bruising on her legs and 'fairy'. Aideen immediately says, 'Oh I bet that's from where she fell on Patrick's bike yesterday.'

Further questioning reveals the following:
- Aideen collected Mo from Joan's on Thursday, and Joan had told Aideen about the accident; Aideen looked after Mo all afternoon
- Aideen saw reddening on Mo's legs when she bathed her and thought she might get a nasty bruise, but as Mo didn't seem to be in pain Aideen didn't think she needed to go to the doctor
- Mo was already in bed when Carl got home on Thursday evening
- Aideen got Mo up in the morning and helped her get dressed
- Carl then took Mo to Joan's
- neither Aideen nor Joan mentioned the bike incident to Carl.

Carl and Aideen agree that Josephine can speak to Mo and ask about what happened. To do so, Josephine sits on the floor with Mo while Aideen sits on the settee. Josephine is very skilled at interviewing children about child protection concerns and manages to encourage Mo to describe how she was 'naughty' and went on Patrick's bike. The bike was also naughty and had made her cry.

Josephine and the police officer feel they have an explanation which reasonably accounts for

Mo's injuries, and the interactions they have seen between child and parents raise no cause for concern. Josephine and the police officer are reassured that there is an accidental explanation for the injuries – though decide to visit Joan's house to have a face-to-face conversation and to see the bike for themselves.

The visit to see Joan confirms that Patrick's bike has a crossbar and is too big for Mo. Patrick also says quite freely that 'Mo was stupid. She hurt herself trying to ride my bike when she's only three. I'm four and bigger.'

Following this visit, Josephine and the police officer consult their seniors, who agree that there does not appear to be any cause for concern about Mo's safety. The following actions are agreed:

▶ Mo will visit the GP on Saturday morning to have her bruises examined
▶ Josephine will advise the out-of-hours GP service about the reason for the medical consultation
▶ the GP will call the out-of-hours social work team to advise of the outcome of the medical consultation
▶ Carl and Aideen will meet Josephine on Monday morning to discuss what the doctor says and to talk through any further need for social services involvement.

The next day, the doctor agrees that Mo's bruising is consistent with the explanation of a bicycle accident. No further injuries are present. On Monday, Carl and Aideen meet with Josephine, who tells them that there is no need for any further action by social services. They discuss all the circumstances of the investigation. Carl and Aideen say they understand why it had happened, but are angry with the nursery for reporting it when they should have known Mo would never be hurt by them. Carl says he is going to take Mo out of the nursery.

▶ If Mo had been at your setting, what information would you require about decisions taken resulting from this investigation?
▶ What could the nursery do now to reassure Carl and Aideen about their role in the investigation, and so encourage them to leave Mo in place?
▶ How would you feel if you were Holly?
▶ Or Cassie?
▶ Or Joan?
▶ Or Carl?
▶ Or Aideen?
▶ Or Mo?

Cassie meets Carl and Aideen

Concerned at Carl's intention to withdraw Mo from the nursery, Josephine arranges a meeting between Cassie and Mo's parents.

Initially, Carl and Aideen say that someone from the nursery – Cassie, Holly, anyone – should have visited Joan and themselves instead of sending social services. Together, Josephine and Cassie explain the nursery's responsibilities regarding child protection, and why they acted as they did in this case. Given all this information, Carl and Aideen then say that they understand why it would not have been right for the nursery to 'investigate'.

Everyone agrees that, in future, they all need to communicate more effectively and make sure all of Mo's carers know crucial information about her, especially during busy and stressful times.

Cassie suggests a 'communication book', in which Aideen, Carl, Joan and the nursery staff can write brief comments about Mo's behaviour and activities. This will give everyone access to what is going on with Mo, and everybody at the meeting thinks this is a good idea.

In the end, Mo remains at the nursery, the relationships between the adults remain positive and there is never any other cause for concern.

10 Supporting individuals

Helping children

Your day-to-day good practice in making and building relationships with young children forms the bedrock of support needed by children who are, or might be, at risk. Listening to children, observing what they do, providing a secure and stable routine, encouraging friendships, celebrating success and offering comfort and support through challenging, confusing and upsetting moments in the normal course of your care are all elements of your work that need to continue at times of stress for a child.

Here are some general pointers to working with children under stress, taken from existing publications (Leach 1992; Webster 2001), which could be helpful for children displaying signs of possible abuse [see Chapter 4].

- **Model good social relationships.** Children at risk, who are being abused or living with violence, experience a great deal of antisocial behaviour. Your general attitude to relationships and behaviour management can offer them more positive experiences. Make it clear that your setting is a place of physical and emotional safety for everybody, talk to the children about respect for others, challenge bullying openly and help children who bully to find other ways of feeling strong. Model the kind of social behaviour you want to encourage, for instance apologise if you realise you have been unfair, and help children put themselves in other people's shoes.
- **Provide security through routine.** A predictable but flexible routine helps children feel that they can rely on some expectations – though a child under great stress may need you to explain and re-explain routines, and may require lots of warning if a routine is to change (eg if you are going on a special outing). Sometimes, children under severe stress will be unable to participate in even the most carefully structured day. In this case, allow them to get on with whatever activity they prefer, keeping them under unobtrusive observation.
- **Make time and space.** At times of stress, children regress in their behaviour, and often need strategies more suited to younger age groups. They may need more adult attention than usual, more praise and approval and lots of 'hands-on' experiences. It is a good idea to cut down on the pressure of adult-directed activities and simply allow the child time and space.
- **Help interaction with other children.** The behaviour of some children under stress may antagonise other children and therefore leave them isolated. When an unsettled child is struggling to get on with peers, you may need to explain to the other children that the child is having a difficult time or is 'unwell' (take care not to give any specific information).

Cuddles and physical affection

As we learn more about child abuse, especially child sexual abuse, people caring for young children tend to worry about touching and playing with them. Young children need close and warm relationships with adults, not just with their own parents but with others who care for them regularly. Cuddles and affection are part of good child care practice.

If you are feeling unsure about whether or not to cuddle a child – and male carers tend to be particularly sensitive about this [see p. 55] – the following points offer some guidance. Touch should:

- be welcomed by the child
- offer a sense of emotional wellbeing and security
- reinforce a sense of positive self-esteem
- support social interaction
- encourage confidence and empowerment
- be in response to a health or welfare concern (Powell 2001).

Children will usually react if you do something they do not like, and then you should stop immediately (as Sally does with Thomas, see case study on page 34). Take notice of what children are telling you through words or behaviour, listen to them and respect their feelings as you would an adult's. Some children seem to be naturally more affectionate and wanting more bodily contact than others. The important thing is not to force attention on a child that he resists or dislikes, and to respond promptly and sensitively to any hint of distress. A parent can probably tell you if a child likes to have his hand held, sit on a lap or receive kisses to his hands, cheeks or head. With babies it is especially important to tune in to their feelings, as they *need* to be held and touched, but have fewer ways of telling you whether they like the way you are doing it or not.

Working with families

Knowledge of a child's family, and good contact with them, are essential for providing any child with effective care. The family assists communication with a child, helps boost her sense of self-worth and increases her confidence in you.

A child should always be seen as an individual, with a particular set of past and present experiences. Determination to remain focused on the child and to consider the entirety of her experiences will enable practitioners to identify children's needs, whatever their background or culture.

Context of a child's upbringing

There are many differences in what people mean by 'family'. Do not make assumptions about what a child's family might be, as it could be very different from yours.

Families might be made up of: mother, father, step-parents, adoptive parents, lesbian and gay co-parents, partners, sisters, brothers, girlfriends, boyfriends, cousins, grandparents, aunts, uncles, family friends, foster carers. Sometimes adults may be ex-partners but still keep in contact with the child and be part of their family, and sometimes they might not have a title. They may be referred to as 'my friend' or just 'Sammy'. These people may be just as significant and play as important a role in the child's life as an aunt or any other traditional family member.

Establishing a good relationship with the family will be good for everyone. Looking after children is rarely straightforward, and will inevitably be as stressful as it is wonderful. If you know a child's family and they know you, they are more likely to ask for your advice and guidance if they are experiencing difficulties. To encourage this situation, you need to offer parents basic information and ask details of them. This can be done by the child's key person or the setting's manager. Childminders may introduce other members of their family at this point. And this process is equally important if you work in a crèche (Pilia 2002).

When you first come into contact with a child, give parents the following information:
► your name
► what you do and your role in the setting as a whole

► the hours during which you will provide care for the child
► arrangements and preferences about food, toys, activities and sleeping pattern
► fees and charging arrangements
► arrangements for giving feedback to parents at the end of a session
► arrangements for parents to offer useful information to setting staff
► the health and safety policy
► how parents may complain
► the safeguarding and behaviour management policy, to include children hurting other children, consequences and rewards
► policy for close physical contact or comforting of children.

At the same time, ask parents to tell you:
► the child's likes and dislikes
► the child's patterns and routines for sleeping, eating and play
► the child's health needs
► the child's behaviour patterns and how behaviours are managed at home
► how the child communicates and what languages are used at home
► any disability or special needs.

Special attention should be paid to the needs of children who do not use English at home and those with a disability or special needs. Useful guidance can be found in Department for Education and Employment 1999, and Dickins & Denziloe 2002.

Child protection policy and discussing concerns with parents

It is recommended that parents are informed of your setting's child protection policy [see 'Drawing up a child protection policy', pp. 58–9]. The NSPCC actively encourages parents to ask for information about child protection procedures and not to assume that every setting is safe.

It is good practice to provide parents with a leaflet or written information on all aspects of the setting, and this should include details of your child protection policy. Such information should be presented in an accessible fashion, but clearly state staff responsibilities regarding child protection. It must also be available to people with different languages or other communication needs due to, for example, disability or being unable to read.

Open discussion about child protection will promote honesty and transparency, and reassure parents that your setting puts the care and safety of their child above all else. It also brings the issue out into the open so that, if you have to talk to a parent about a concern, it will not be the first time you have discussed child protection. This may make your task easier if the parent is angry at you for questioning him or if he questions you about a concern he has regarding a member of staff, as you can refer him to the earlier discussion. If this is not enough, here are some useful strategies for dealing with angry family members:

▸ try to ensure that there is another member of staff nearby and that you have a way out of the room if necessary
▸ accept parents' feelings rather than denying them or getting angry yourself
▸ quietly remind them of your responsibility to safeguard all children – make reference to the procedures, if appropriate
▸ show concern for parents: 'This must be a painful time for you too'
▸ stay calm, restrain your own feelings, and share them with a trusted colleague or adviser as soon as possible.

When discussing a child protection concern, parents are likely to feel scared or guilty, so you can reassure them about the child protection processes and systems used by social services and the police. It may transpire that the family requires support services: extra sessions, behaviour management advice, health advice, etc [see 'Support for families in need', below].

Some of the questions parents might ask you about child protection and abuse are likely to be similar to those you had before learning more about safeguarding children. This is another reason to ensure that everyone in your setting has some awareness about child protection.

You may think that open discussion is easier said than done, but child protection should be seen as an everyday part of looking after children.

Support for families in need

Research has looked into the influence of parenting 'style' and the quality of attachment on incidences of child abuse [see 'Relationships and attachment', p. 14]. While there are many aspects to being a parent, the following four styles of parenting have been identified:

▸ authoritative – warm but firm
▸ authoritarian – emphasises obedience and conformity
▸ indulgent – accepting of most behaviours
▸ indifferent – life and discipline is centred on adult's needs and, if extreme, is neglectful (Steinberg 1993).

Many factors influence an adult's parenting style, but research concludes that children who experience poor communication, hostility, low commitment and negative contact in relationships with their parents are likely to suffer social, emotional, educational and employment difficulties (Schaffer 1996; Steinberg 1993). It has also shown that a combination of low warmth and high criticism can be abusive (Department of Health 1995).

Socio-economic factors such as unemployment, money problems and poor housing, education or health can affect parent–child relationships. For example, children who live in poor-quality damp housing may be more demanding because they feel constantly cold and uncomfortable. This may elicit a different type of relationship with their parents than if they lived in adequate housing where they were warm and comfortable.

Parenting affected by domestic violence, mental health and alcohol or drug abuse can adversely affect children and be a predetermining factor for abuse [see 'Mental illness, substance abuse and domestic violence, p. 15]. In its extreme form, poor parenting can be abusive.

There are several national organisations that offer parenting education and support [see Appendix 2], and many local ones too. You can find a comprehensive list of organisations by visiting the National Family and Parenting Institute (NFPI) website at www.nfpi.org, and going to its 'Parent Services Directory'.

Stresses and difficulties experienced by families can be reduced by effective support services, and this can play a major role in preventing abuse (National Commission of Inquiry into the Prevention of Child Abuse 1996). Support should aim to offer help at the right time, come from the right people and be in the right place, and can be offered by a range of bodies, both professional and voluntary. The kind of parenting support that has been found to reduce the likelihood of abuse and improve child outcomes includes:

▸ early intervention, either home-based or centre-based
▸ a duration of at least six months and possibly up to several years
▸ support offered close to (or before) the birth of a baby
▸ intense support, offered at least once a week, if not more frequently

▶ comprehensive input, not just focusing on parenting skills

▶ help offered by workers whose personality is warm and accepting (Daniel, Wassell & Gilligan 1999).

Support will only be effective if it is appropriate for an individual family and offered to them in a way that encourages them to take it up. Parents may then feel able to change their parenting style – if this is seen to be causing difficulties – as they know that someone is there to help.

Social services offer families a lot of assistance, but in some cases they may be unable to provide support because resources are already allocated or because they may simply not be the right agency to do so (Parton 1997).

Do not underestimate small steps and small achievements when encouraging parents experiencing difficulty to take up services that will be useful to them. Just ten minutes of one-to-one contact with a non-communicative parent may help build trust and encourage communication with you. This may help you identify difficulties that the family is having, and allow you to consider any practical support that you can genuinely offer (an extra session, a home visit from the child's key person, an invitation to attend your parents' consultation evening) or to call other agencies for advice about different services that the family may need. If you work in a Sure Start programme, or are housed in an Early Excellence Centre or family centre, there is likely to be a number of good family support services close at hand.

There are also a number of family centres, some run by large child care agencies like NCH and Barnardo's, which focus on providing support to families with a child on the child protection register, on behalf of social services. This kind of centre has appropriately qualified professionals on site who can provide more targeted help (Lloyd 1996).

A different kind of support is provided by Home-Start volunteers, who visit families in their own homes, usually once a week for between two and four hours. The visits are flexible, and the volunteer and family decide together when they should take place, and how much time should be spent. Volunteers might be called upon simply to listen to parents, or to offer practical support such as playing with the children – much as a friend would. For many families, this simple type of support can make a world of difference.

If you are not sure what kind of help is available to families in your area, contact your local authority and check the NFPI website's Parent Services Directory (www.nfpi.org). Please also see Appendix 2 at the end of this book.

Support for practitioners and other adults

Male practitioners

The majority of convicted people who have offended against children are men. This, compounded by the media's often hysterical and provocative approach to the capture, trial or release of paedophiles, has created a sense of insecurity among some parents towards male child carers. It has also made it more difficult for men to be confident, caring early years practitioners as they may fear allegations of abuse.

Other European countries do not harbour the same suspicion against men in early years settings, and show what an important part they can play in helping children grow up free from gender stereotypes (Cameron, Moss & Owen 1999). Careful introduction of male carers to parents and other practitioners can help them all feel more at ease. A willingness to discuss openly both the benefits of and concerns raised by men in the nursery, and involvement of male carers in those discussions, can help to reinforce that ease. Both strategies are consistent with having good, strong policies aimed at protecting children from risk [see Chapter 11].

Practitioners working with a child who has been abused

The emotional impact of dealing with child abuse is a very real problem for most adults who come into contact with abused or neglected children. Child abuse, especially child sexual abuse, can arouse strong emotions in adults. Feelings of revulsion and anger are quite normal. If you know the child well this can be a particularly difficult time for you. It is important to find help and support for yourself in coping with your feelings, or you may find that you begin to have problems in dealing with other children and families, including your own.

These feelings can take different forms. You may become very preoccupied with the particular case, or feel that you are in conflict with another agency or professional worker. You may become preoccupied with the general subject of child abuse and feel that every child you see or come into contact with has been abused. You might become very upset or emotional when reading a newspaper or watching television if cases of child abuse are featured. All of these reactions are very common. It is important to share these feelings with informed and sympathetic listeners. Your family, friends or colleagues are a good starting point, as they will be able to give you personal, if not professional, support.

You should also be able to turn to a senior colleague, a social services department or the NSPCC for advice and help. For reasons of confidentiality, you will not want to talk about details that identify the child, but you can still talk about how the case makes you feel.

If you have made a referral because you suspect that a child has been abused, then you have done the right thing. You should hold on to that fact and keep it in your mind during the following few weeks. You have helped to ensure the protection of a vulnerable member of society who may be at risk of harm.

It is recommended that the management of child care services includes the regular supervision and appraisal of staff. Supervision is often a one-to-one meeting with your line manager where all aspects of your work and job are discussed. These meetings can therefore provide an opportunity to raise any concerns or queries you may have about child protection issues, and to receive support. They can also provide an opportunity to identify and agree on any training you may need about safeguarding children and child protection. There are many organisations that provide such training. These include Area Child Protection Committees, social services, the NSPCC and the National Early Years Network.

By the time a child abuse case reaches the stage where action is being taken, it is very likely that other members of staff will be aware that 'something is going on'. While the details of a case should not be disclosed under any circumstances, it may be necessary to let staff know that the setting is involved in a case of abuse, especially as they may be approached by parents who have heard rumours and want some information. Careful thought should be given to exactly how and when staff are informed, and again emphasis should be placed on the need for professionalism, confidentiality, sensitivity and discretion.

Parents of other children

If the setting is involved in some way in a child protection investigation, staff and volunteers should be given guidance about how to respond if they are approached by families of other children. Rumours and gossip are inevitable, so managers need to agree with staff and volunteers on a common approach about what to tell parents of other children, and how best to go about it. Specific information about an incident will be confidential, so details given to other parents must be kept to a minimum. Parents should be advised that the issue is being dealt with in line with the setting's policy. Everyone should be reassured that concerns are being dealt with appropriately and further questions should be directed to a manager or senior staff member. For advice and guidance about informing parents regarding a specific case, contact the child protection agencies involved (social services, police, NSPCC).

The non-abusing parent or carer

If the person suspected of abuse is one of the child's parents, there will almost certainly be other people in the child's life who will be upset and confused about what has happened. They may need information and advice, or might just want someone to talk to. In the longer term, they are likely to play an important role in helping the child recover from the experience of abuse. Depending on the nature of your relationship with them, it might be best to refer them to another agency for help, for example the Family Rights Group or local Family Service Unit. In any case, they should not be forgotten and it is important to be as helpful, sensitive and supportive to them as possible.

More than one family involved in an incident

A situation which involves more than one child or family may be particularly difficult to manage, especially with regard to sharing information, for example where a child is allegedly being abused by another child's father. The principles of confidentiality and record-keeping must be maintained. The most important factor for all involved is to remain child-focused. In a case like this, judgements about an adult's guilt or responsibility should be avoided when considering whether both children should still attend the nursery. The main consideration is to provide a safe and supportive environment for the children, so the assessment and management of risk is tantamount. The investigating agencies will be able to advise you, for example, on whether the alleged perpetrator should be allowed to come to the nursery. The children involved may need to be offered alternate sessions to avoid conflict or contaminating any evidence.

Allegations against early years practitioner

Although the child protection process remains the same if a practitioner is under suspicion of abuse, other factors come into play. All settings and registration bodies, *eg* Ofsted, have procedures which must be followed when allegations are made against practitioners. Such allegations require special attention, as the risks, the circumstances of the allegation and the nature of the setting or service's work all need to be taken into account. Procedures should cross-reference to disciplinary procedures [see Chapter 11].

An allegation may mean that the person puts children at risk and that immediate safeguards should be put into place to reduce this risk. This might involve:

▶ suspension from work entirely
▶ allocation of different duties that do not involve direct contact with children
▶ being paired or shadowed by another practitioner while the investigation takes place (the individual who will shadow in this way should be identified in a setting's child protection policy and be trained in supervision).

If the child protection investigation concludes that the person has perpetrated child abuse, assessment of future risk and possible criminal proceedings will influence whether she is safe to work with children in the future. If the investigation does not support the allegation the person may be considered safe to continue in her role. However, investigations may be inconclusive and may raise concerns about a person's suitability to work with children. This eventuality should be provided for in the setting's disciplinary and competence procedures, which will act as a preventative factor against risk of abuse in a setting [see Chapter 11].

11 Child protection policies and procedures

Following the Care Standards Act 2000, all early years settings must have child protection procedures in place if they are to meet the national standards for registration. There is no point having procedures if they are not applicable to a specific setting, so rather than provide a sample child protection policy (which might not work for your circumstances), the section 'Drawing up a child protection policy', below, raises the issues and general principles that you need to consider when writing your policy. The section 'Other relevant procedures' shows how a number of other policies and procedures support the child protection policy.

Drawing up a child protection policy

Making preparations

First of all, contact your local Area Child Protection Committee (ACPC). This is a body made up of all the agencies involved in protecting children, including social services, health, police, education, and sometimes the NSPCC and other voluntary groups. Local child protection procedures and practices are developed through this committee. You can obtain a copy of the local guidelines for child protection policies and advice about how your ACPC might assist you from your local social services department. Some ACPCs provide training and development support for local projects and groups.

When it comes to actually thinking about your child protection policy, it is useful first of all to establish some general details. Write down or gather together the following information about your setting or service:

► aims and objectives
► staff structure and number of workers (both paid staff and volunteers)
► affiliation, if any, to a national organisation or umbrella group
► current child protection policy and procedures, and other relevant procedures [see pp. 59–60]
► motivation for writing/rewriting child protection policy at this time (eg a specific incident, a request from Ofsted).

Writing the policy statement

The policy statement provides everyone in the early years setting or service – practitioners, parents and children – with a declaration of the principles that guide your child protection policy. It should:

► identify the early years setting or service and state its purpose or function
► recognise the responsibility of the setting or service to safeguard all young children in its care
► state the setting's or service's position and responsibilities in relation to both child abuse and child protection
► recognise the needs of children from minority ethnic groups, and those with disabilities, and state that the policies and procedures apply to all children, regardless of gender, ethnicity, disability, sexuality, religion or culture (and regardless of those of their parents)
► cite the national or international principles, legislation and guidance underpinning the policy (eg the Children Act 1989, the UN Convention on the Rights of the Child, the Care Standards Act 2000)
► briefly refer to associated guidance or procedures (eg equal opportunities legislation).

Implementing the policy

A policy statement, while vital, can achieve little or nothing without an associated implementation strategy. This is where the precise details of how the principles given in the policy statement are translated into action. The strategy should include the following information:

1 The name of the person who is responsible for child protection in the setting or service, with contact numbers for when that person is not on site.
2 Contact numbers for the duty child protection team in the local social services department.
3 The process that individual practitioners should follow if:
   - they think a child may be being abused by someone either in the setting or elsewhere
   - a child discloses abuse
   - there are concerns or allegations about the behaviour (current or in the past) of a member of staff or volunteer towards the children.
4 Details of how allegations or concerns about specific incidents of abuse are to be recorded and kept confidential.

5 A written code of behaviour outlining good practice when working with children. This should make a statement about positive physical contact; something which recognises that, as young children require lots of physical contact – when being comforted or read to or, in the case of babies, simply when being fed – practitioners will touch and hug them as part of their daily care. This must be balanced with guidance about behaviour that is inappropriate, starting with behaviour that children themselves reject. Specifically, the code of behaviour could cover bullying, racism, controlling anger, responding to aggression, intimate care tasks (changing nappies, visiting the toilet with children), appropriate and inappropriate touching, sexual behaviour, and working with colleagues and parents.

6 The process by which the policy's implementation will be monitored, identifying what can be measured, by whom, how and when, and the criteria for determining success.

7 Details of the possible blocks to successful implementation, and ways that these can be overcome.

8 Details of how practitioners, parents and children (where appropriate and in keeping with their stage of development) will receive information about the policy itself.

9 A training plan and regular opportunities for all practitioners to learn about child protection and about health and safety. Under the Day Care Standards, child protection training must be supplied to at least one designated member of staff, and all new members of staff must be given induction training on the setting's child protection policies and procedures in their first week. It is also important that the staff's knowledge of child protection procedures is regularly updated through appropriate training (Ofsted 2001).

Good reporting structures are crucial. When developing policies and procedures, it is essential to be sure that the people with decision-making responsibility for child protection will fully support the setting's staff. Depending on how your setting is organised, the management committee, trustees and directors must mandate, endorse and support the proposals to develop a child protection strategy, and provide the incentive and resources to carry it out. The changes recommended by the strategy may result in changes to procedures and practice for your setting when dealing with issues of child protection. Some of these may be disruptive, and staff will find it easier to take the strategy forward if they receive open encouragement and approval from their managers. [See also box 'Procedures for reporting concerns', p. 33.]

Other relevant procedures

Safeguarding children's welfare and protection is only one element of an effective child protection policy. Other policies and procedures can also assist in protecting children, all of which should be monitored and reviewed regularly to ensure that they are still applicable, effective and up to date with any changes in legislation or guidance. Information about the law and guidance on good practice for most of the following policies and procedures can be found in *Good to work for* (Reason 1998).

Good employment practice

Good employment practice, with regular supervision by line managers, offers constant support to practitioners and is key for those who are working with children involved in child protection procedures.

Whistleblowing/speak-out policy

Under the Public Interest Disclosure Act 1998, individuals cannot be disciplined for speaking out against a colleague or employer. A whistleblowing policy promotes the disclosure by a staff member of confidential information relating to some danger, fraud, or other illegal or unethical conduct connected with or influential to the workplace.

Confidentiality policy

This policy deals with maintaining the confidentiality of individuals once a child protection concern has been raised, and also the procedures for dealing with information that has been supplied 'in confidence'.

Equal opportunities policy

Within child protection there are issues of stereotypes, myths and value systems which may influence a person's actions regarding concerns about children. An equal opportunities policy provides a mechanism to raise staff awareness, and also to promote principles that all children – regardless of their ethnicity, class, age, sexuality, gender, religion or disability – have equal rights to protection from harm.

Complaints and grievance policy

An issue may arise regarding an employee's conduct that does not call for action within a child protection policy but which is of sufficient concern to warrant action by management (*eg* a complaint by a parent about offensive language used by an employee) and must be dealt with by some formal action. Clear, well-advertised processes for dealing with complaints or grievances will give parents and carers greater confidence that the setting is committed to providing safe, good-quality services.

Disciplinary policy and procedures

A code of conduct and details of good practice dictate appropriate and acceptable behaviour. Their existence can help minimise the opportunity for abuse and reduce the likelihood for allegations or false accusations. Principles of good practice should exist with regard to

- physical comfort
- feeding
- bullying
- controlling anger
- responding to aggression
- possession of knives and weapons
- compensation for injury
- intimate care tasks
- appropriate and inappropriate touching
- sexual behaviour
- working together
- relationships of trust
- smoking
- alcohol and drug use
- transport.

The code of conduct must be accompanied by a regulatory system so that staff, parents and children know what may happen if they do not follow the guidelines.

Information technology

There should be guidance about misuse of the Internet and awareness of access to pornography or other unacceptable sites. NCH provides useful guidance on this issue via its NCH IT OK website (www.nch.org. uk/itok) and other publications (NCH 2001a; 2001b).

Outings

Guidance on policy for the staffing and management of outings is available from the Department for Education and Skills, and from the Health and Safety Executive (Department for Education and Employment 1998; Health and Safety Executive 1998; 1999).

think

Individually, or as a team, explore your knowledge and views of your setting with regard to safeguarding children.

- Which policies and procedures are effective in promoting the safeguarding of children?
- How does a setting support practitioners in making certain that such policies are acted upon in daily practice?
- Are there any policies or procedures which act as a barrier to safeguarding children?
- Are there developments which might promote or increase child protection?

Contact other groups or local settings to find out about the procedures they have which promote safeguarding and about their child protection policies, then repeat this exercise.

Appendix 1 **The legal framework**

A range of laws, government guidance and standards determine and shape child protection systems and practices. These have been developed through experience and research into how best to protect children (Department of Health 1995), and provide a framework for agencies which offer services to children and families, to ensure their safety and wellbeing.

The main legislation that determines the duties of the local authority (and others) to provide services for children in need and to protect children from harm is The Children Act 1989, which legislates for the care and protection of children in England and Wales. The Children (Northern Ireland) Order 1995 and The Children (Scotland) Act 1995 maintain the same principles.

The Children Act 1989

This law is founded on the assumption that it is generally best for children to grow up in their own families, and that most parents want to care for their children without interference from others. However, the local authority may need to provide services for children who need assistance or protection.

Local authorities have a legal duty to provide services for children identified as being 'in need', to promote their welfare and to protect them from abuse. The responsibility for investigating child protection concerns lies with social services and the police. The NSPCC is also authorised within the Act (Order) to take action to protect children.

However, the Children Act (Section 27) and subsequent government guidance (Department of Health *et al.* 1999) also state that education, health, housing and community services all have roles and responsibilities in protecting children. If a concern is reported to social services they have to provide a response and ensure that it is properly investigated.

In its 'welfare checklist', The Children Act 1989 states that social workers and decisions taken by courts should take account of the following:

▶ 'the ascertainable wishes and feelings of the child concerned (considered in light of his age and understanding)
▶ his physical, emotional and educational needs

▶ the likely effect on him of any change in circumstances
▶ his age, sex, background and any characteristics of his wishes which the court considers relevant
▶ any harm which he has suffered or is at risk of suffering
▶ how capable each of his parents, and any other person in relation to whom the court considers the question to be relevant, is of meeting his needs
▶ the range of powers available to the court under this Act in the proceedings in question' (Children Act 1989, para 1.3).

In practice, the checklist means that any child protection intervention has to, for example:

▶ plan contact with family and friends if the child does have to be removed
▶ ensure that health needs are met
▶ make sure that the child's cultural and religious needs are met
▶ ensure that the child receives education.

The focus on a child's safety means there is often tension and a fast turn of events during a child protection investigation. Nevertheless, it is crucial that the aspects listed on the welfare checklist are considered. You may already know some of this information about a child and be able to ensure that social services are aware of all the details. This will assist not only the social services and parents but make the process less traumatic for the child. It may be that a nursery place can be instantly extended or that you can be flexible enough so that the child can continue attending the setting even though her home circumstances have changed. Family centres or Early Excellence Centres can sometimes offer familiar, neutral and safe spaces for children to have contact with their families. The social services department may ask you about the possibility of this happening where you work, but it is important that the child's need to have her usual 'nursery' experience should not be compromised.

Section 17

Section 17 of the Children Act 1989 places a duty on local authorities to provide services for 'children in need'. A child may be 'in need' when:

▶ 'he is unlikely to achieve or maintain, or to have the opportunity of achieving or maintaining, a reasonable standard of health or development without the provision for him of services by a local authority

- his health or development is likely to be significantly impaired, or further impaired, without the provision for him of such services
- he is disabled'.

This section of the law does not mean families must accept support services or intervention from social services. It places an obligation on the local authority to identify, assess and respond to a need for services.

So when is it legally possible to protect children ...?

Section 47

Under Section 47 (1b) of the Children Act 1989 a local authority has a duty to investigate where they 'have reasonable cause to suspect that a child who lives, or is found, in their area is suffering, or is likely to suffer, significant harm'.

Social services, the police, the court and the NSPCC can legally intervene in order to protect a child only if the child is suffering, or likely to suffer, significant harm.

The Children Act 1989 does not use the term 'child abuse'. Instead it uses the words 'significant harm'. There is no definition of significant harm in the Children Act, but the accepted interpretation of 'harm' is broad and includes:

- ill-treatment
- the impairment of health
- the impairment of development (whether physical, intellectual, emotional, social or behavioural).

Everyone will have their own interpretation of what they think is harmful for a child, although significant harm has been roughly summarised under four categories of 'abuse' [see pp. 8–9]. All children are different, their situations are different, their experiences of abuse are different and to begin to protect them we have to recognise them as individuals with rights as human beings. Otherwise, child protection agencies might assume that what protects one child will protect every child and be in every child's best interests.

Working together to safeguard children

This government guidance deals with inter-agency work and specifically includes the roles and responsibilities of community services in the protection of children (Department of Health et al. 1999). It says that agencies such as schools, health centres, nurseries, the police and social services all have to 'work together', talk to each other and support each other in promoting children's welfare.

This guidance has helped to ensure that police and social workers are trained together on how best to investigate suspicions or allegations of child abuse.

Framework for the assessment of children in need and their families

Since the introduction of the Children Act 1989, government policy has emphasised the importance of partnership with parents and favoured family support services. The document *Child protection: messages from research* collated critical pieces of research, the findings of which contributed to further child protection measures (Department of Health 1995). One finding was that children are almost always better off in their own homes, and this resulted in the 'refocusing' of resources towards greater support for families.

This approach assists the prevention of child abuse and, in the longer term, promotes children's welfare. Its value was confirmed in a review of recent studies on the Children Act (Aldgate & Statham 2001), though one of these studies (Thoburn, Wilding & Watson 2000) noted that, in many child protection cases involving children under eight, assessment was based on risk rather than need, and that needs remained unmet.

Framework for the assessment of children in need and their families (Department of Health et al. 2000) is a key element of the government's Quality Protects programme, which aims to transform the management and delivery of children's services so that vulnerable children are given better life chances. The framework provides a systematic way of assessing children and families across three inter-related areas, called domains, each with a range of specific areas that should be addressed. The three domains are:

- the child's development needs
- parental capacity to respond to the needs of the child
- wider family and environmental factors.

The framework is child-centred and rooted in child development. Social services and other agencies contributing to the assessment have to work within clearly defined timescales and provide an analysis of a child's needs in order to determine the services required by the family. It is used in association with *Working together to safeguard children* (Department of Health *et al.* 1999) so that where there are concerns that a child may be, or is, suffering significant harm, professionals will follow consistent guidance.

Human Rights Act 1998 *and*

United Nations Convention on the Rights of the Child (UNCRC)

The 1998 Act and the Convention that was ratified by the UK Government in 1991 both reflect principles that are recognised in UK legislation and in International Agreements. However, only the Act has any legal force, and it can actually discriminate against children to some extent, as it can be seen to prioritise parents' rights over those of children.

Despite its lack of legal force, the UNCRC has been adopted by 90 local authorities, which aim to uphold its principles, that:

► the welfare and protection of children is paramount, whatever the circumstances

► all children, regardless of age, disability, gender, racial heritage, religious belief and sexual orientation or identity have the right to protection from all types of harm and abuse.

The Convention's 54 sections are called articles, and these have informed and shaped government initiatives such as Sure Start (Thompson 1999). In relation to child protection, Article 19 reads:

1 States Parties shall take all appropriate legislative, administrative, social and educational measures to protect the child from all forms of physical or mental violence, injury or abuse, neglect or negligent treatment, maltreatment or exploitation, including sexual abuse, while in the care of parent(s), legal guardian(s) or any other person who has the care of the child

2 Such protective measures should, as appropriate, include effective procedures for the establishment of social programmes to provide necessary support for the child and for those who have the care of the child, as well as for other forms of prevention and for identification, reporting, referral, investigation, treatment and follow-up of instances of child maltreatment described heretofore, and, as appropriate, for judicial involvement.

Criminal Justice and Courts Services Act 2000 Part II

This Act relates to the responsibilities of 'public bodies' for child protection. It is integral to child protection systems in the UK and links to other laws, including the Protection of Children Act 1999 and the Police Act 1997 [see below], which together build a system that:

► defines jobs and positions that are 'regulated' – anyone identified as inappropriate to work with children should not seek or be given these jobs

► makes it a criminal offence if employers do not take sufficient steps to check employees working with children and/or knowingly appoints an employee who has a disqualification order against him as a consequence of committing an offence against a child – employers are criminally liable if they appoint someone to a regulated position

► makes it a criminal offence for convicted sex offenders to seek employment, or be appointed to work, with children – sex offenders, as disqualified persons, are criminally liable if they seek employment with children.

Protection of Children Act 1999 *and*

Police Act 1997

Taken together, these two Acts make it possible for employers to check whether a potential or actual employee has criminal offences against children or whether there has been reason for that person to be considered inappropriate to work with children.

The Protection of Children Act (PoCA) 1999 places a duty on the Secretary of State for Health to compile a list of people considered to be unsuitable to work with children. This is known as the PoCA List. Both this list and another, the Department for Education and Skills (DfES) List 99 include adults who, due to lack of evidence, have not been convicted of causing significant harm, but who gave the authorities cause to be concerned about child safety during a child protection investigation. The DfES List 99 lists nurses or teachers who are considered inappropriate to work with children.

The PoCA 1999 builds a framework for a cross-sector scheme to identify those people considered to be unsuitable to work with children, including a statutory requirement for all 'child care organisations' to:

- refer names, in a given set of circumstances, for possible inclusion on the PoCA List
- check against the PoCA List and the DfES List 99 when proposing to appoint someone to a child care position
- not employ a person in a child care position if that person is included on the PoCA List or DfES List 99
- cease to employ someone in a child care position if it is discovered that the individual is on the PoCA List or DfES List 99.

There are differences between statutory child care organisations which are 'regulated' and other organisations that also 'care' for children in some way. The provisions of the PoCA 1999 are not mandatory for the latter organisations but it is the government's hope that they will take advantage of the scheme to its fullest extent in order to ensure that they provide a comparable level of safety to children in their care. Thus all 'other' organisations are encouraged to refer names to the Secretary of State for consideration of inclusion in the PoCA List and to check against the List when proposing to appoint people to child care positions.

The Act sets out the circumstances where a child care organisation must, and other organisations *may*, refer names to the Secretary of State for consideration of inclusion in the PoCA List. These are that:

1 'the organisation has dismissed the individual on the grounds of misconduct (whether or not in the course of employment) which harmed a child or placed a child at risk of harm
2 the individual has resigned or retired in circumstances such that the organisation would have dismissed him, or would have considered dismissing him on such grounds if he had not resigned or retired
3 the organisation has, on such grounds, transferred the individual to a position within the organisation which is not a child care position
4 the organisation has, on such grounds, suspended the individual or provisionally transferred him to such a position as in (3) above, but has not yet decided whether to dismiss him or to confirm the transfer'.

A name may also be referred if information comes to the organisation's attention where the person is no longer with them, when on the basis of that information the organisation would have, or would have considered, dismissing him on the grounds of misconduct which harmed a child or placed a child at risk of harm (Home Office 2000b).

In anticipation of the PoCA 1999 and the Police Act 1997, Part V, the Home Office has set up the Criminal Records Bureau (CRB). This is a 'one-stop-shop' for checking police records, criminal conviction records, the PoCA List and DfES List 1999. Statutory services, voluntary groups, charities, sporting bodies, and any agency providing services or working with children, will be able to use the CRB. There are significant rules and regulations about the use of the CRB so you may want to explore further how your workplace or situation may use it (the CRB information line is on 0870 90 90 811).

Data Protection Acts 1984 and 1998

These two Acts regulate what information can be shared, and with whom. If reports are made on children and families to any agency then they have to consider who will be told, who has access to the record, how the information will be stored and passed on, and by whom. The main effect on child protection is that:

- records have to be kept securely
- only certain people should be able to access that information
- if the information relates to child protection it cannot be withheld, as this would not be in the child's best interests
- families, individuals and children can see most of what is recorded about them and have an opportunity to respond

The system and procedure for recording material relating to child protection in your setting should comply with requirements under the Data Protection Act. This is also reassuring for anyone reporting concerns, so they know that the information they give has to be managed sensitively by law.

Family Law Act 1996

The Family Law Act 1996 makes many provisions with respect to divorce and separation. The main influences on child protection are:

- a non-abusing parent can maintain tenancy of a home even if she is not legally the owner, on grounds of the interests of the child
- an adult experiencing violence from a partner can obtain an order preventing the partner from coming to the home or from assaulting her.

There is a range of powers available under the Family Law Act 1996 which may allow the perpetrator to be removed from the family home instead of removing a child. For the court to include an exclusion requirement in a child protection order, it must be satisfied that:

► there is reasonable cause to believe that the child will cease to suffer, or to be likely to suffer, significant harm if the person is excluded from the home in which the child lives

► another person living in the home is able and willing to give the child the care which it would be reasonable to expect a parent to give, and consents to the exclusion requirement.

Historically, women may not have reported abuse or violence to themselves or the children from fear of being made homeless. This Act gives them and their children increased protection.

Sex Offenders Act 1997

This Act instructs those who have been convicted of a sexual offence against children to register their address with the police. If they do not, they can be fined or imprisoned. People convicted prior to 1997 do not have to register.

Care Standards Act 2000, Part VI *and*

National Standards for Under Eights Day Care and Childminding

Ofsted's Early Years Directorate is responsible for the registration, regulation and inspection of all early years provision, whether it is care or education. It delivers its services through national functions, a regional structure and a local presence. Registered providers have to meet 14 regulated national minimum standards of quality for services to children under eight years (Department for Education and Employment 2001).

The standards apply to quality in full day care, childminding, crèches, out-of-school care and sessional care, and include the following.

► **Section 11, Behaviour:** Adults caring for children in the provision are able to manage a wide range of children's behaviour in a way which promotes their welfare and development.

► **Section 13, Child protection:** The registered person complies with local child protection procedures approved by the Area Child Protection Committee and ensures that all adults working and looking after children in the provision are able to put the procedures into practice.

There are additional criteria for the care of babies.

The national standards were introduced in 2001, and one of their practical benefits will be to reduce risk to children as they are enforceable and mandatory.

Providers who do not meet the minimum standards may:

► be refused registration
► have their registration cancelled
► have conditions of registration imposed on them
► have existing conditions varied.

Early years providers can object to Ofsted's decisions relating to child protection and ultimately have a 'right of appeal' which will be heard by a tribunal established under the Protection of Children Act 1999.

Appendix 2 **Useful contacts**

Child protection

ChildLine
2nd floor
Royal Mail Buildings
50 Studd Street
London W1 0QW
helpline 0800 1111
website www.childline.org.uk
Free, 24-hour helpline for children and young people in trouble or danger.

Children 1st
41 Polwarth Terrace
Edinburgh EH11 1NU
tel 0131 337 8539
website www.children1st.org.uk
Children 1st is the Royal Scottish Society for the Prevention of Cruelty to Children. Its work is similar to that of the NSPCC in England and Wales, as it supports families under stress, protects children from harm and neglect, helps children recover from abuse, and promotes children's rights and interests.

Criminal Records Bureau
PO Box 110
Liverpool L3 677
tel 0870 90 90 811
website www.crb.gov.uk
An executive agency of the Home Office which helps organisations make safer recruitment decisions. Their 'disclosure' service helps employers in the public, private and voluntary sectors identify candidates who may be unsuitable for certain work, especially that involving contact with children or other vulnerable members of society.

Kidscape
2 Grosvenor Gardens
London SW1W 0DH
tel 020 7730 3300
website www.kidscape.org.uk
This national charity aims to keep children safe from harm by focusing on preventative tactics to use before abuse takes place and producing practical resources for children, parents, teachers, social workers and community workers.

National Society for the Prevention of Cruelty to Children (NSPCC)
42 Curtain Road
London EC2A 3NH
tel 020 7825 2500
helpline 0808 800 5000
website www.nspcc.org.uk
The UK's leading charity specialising in child protection and the prevention of cruelty to children.

Support for children and families

Children's Legal Centre
University of Essex
Wivenhoe Park
Colchester CO4 3SQ
tel 01206 873820
website www2.essex.ac.uk/clc
Independent national charity concerned with law and policy affecting children and young people. Legal queries can be emailed via a form on their website.

Contact-a-Family
209–211 City Road
London EC1V 1JN
tel 020 7608 8700
helpline 0808 808 3555
website www.cafamily.org.uk
Brings together families which have a disabled child. Has information on hundreds of support groups associated with disabilities and conditions, including rare and unusual ones. Website includes downloadable factsheets on a range of special needs issues. CaF also runs a national helpline for parents.

Families Need Fathers
134 Curtain Road
London EC2A 3AR
tel 020 7613 5060
website www.fnf.org.uk
A UK charity which provides information and support to parents – of either sex – and is chiefly concerned with the problems of maintaining a child's relationship with both parents during and after family breakdown.

Family Rights Group
The Print House
18 Ashwin Street
London E8 3DL
tel 020 7923 2628
website www.frg.org.uk
A group of social workers, lawyers and others who want to improve law and practice relating to children in care. Includes an advice service for families with children in care.

Family Service Units
207 Old Marylebone Road
London NW1 5QP
tel 020 7402 5175
website www.fsu.org.uk
Provides service and support for disadvantaged families and communities in over 20 areas in the UK. Aims to prevent family and community breakdown.

Family Welfare Association
501–505 Kingsland Road
London E8 4AU
tel 020 7254 6251
FamilyLine 020 7923 9200
Support and funding for distressed and disadvantaged families in London, Milton Keynes and Nottingham. National confidential phone helpline on grants and financial support.

Gingerbread
7 Sovereign Close
Sovereign Court
London E1W 3HW
tel 020 7488 9300
helpline 0800 018 4318
website www.gingerbread.org.uk
Supports lone parents and their children with financial, social and legal advice, and through social and practical activities. There are over 300 local self-help groups.

Home-Start
2 Salisbury Road
Leicester LE1 7QR
tel 08000 68 63 68
website www.home-start.org.uk
National organisation supporting Home-Start schemes which provide trained parent volunteers to help any parent of pre-school children who is finding it hard to cope. Volunteers visit parents in their own homes. Home-Start is established in over 300 communities across the UK and with British Forces abroad.

National Association of Child Contact Centres
Minerva House
Spaniel Row
Nottingham NG1 6EP
tel 0115 948 4557
website www.naccc.org.uk
A charity that provides neutral venues where the children of separated families can enjoy contact with one – or both – parents, and sometimes other family members, in a comfortable and safe environment when there is no viable alternative.

National Childbirth Trust
Alexandra House
Oldham Terrace
London W3 6NH
tel 0870 444 8707
website www.nctpregnancyandbabycare.com
Offers information, advice and support on pregnancy, childbirth, child development and the first months of parenthood.

National Drugs Helpline
tel 0800 77 66 00
website www.ndh.org.uk
A helpline offering information and advice to anyone concerned about drugs, including drug users, their families, friends and people who work with them.

National Family Mediation (NFM)
104–108 Grafton Road
London NW5 4BD
tel 020 7485 8809
website www.nfm.u-net.com
A network of over 60 local not-for-profit family mediation services in England and Wales offering help to couples, married or unmarried, who are in the process of separation and divorce. Mediators help clients reach joint decisions about the issues associated with their separation – children, finance and property – and several NFM services also provide specialist services for children.

National Newpin (New Parent Information Network)
Sutherland House
35 Sutherland Square
London SE17 3EE
tel 020 7358 5900
website www.newpin.org.uk
Offers parents and children an opportunity to achieve positive changes in their lives and relationships, and to break the cycle of destructive family behaviour. There are 15 centres, mainly in the London area. Newpin offers parenting skills training programmes and includes a fathers' project.

NHS Direct
helpline 0845 46 47
website www.nhsdirect.nhs.uk
A 24-hour nurse advice and health information service, providing confidential information on what to do if someone is feeling ill, particular health conditions, local healthcare services and local support organisations.

Parentline Plus
Unit 529, Highgate Studios
53–79 Highgate Road
London NW5 1TL
tel 020 7284 5500
helpline 0808 800 2222
website www.parentlineplus.org.uk
Formed following the merger of Parentline and the National Stepfamily Association. Supports anyone parenting a child including grandparents and foster parents. Runs a freephone helpline and courses for parents, and has a range of downloadable information on the website.

Parentline Scotland
c/o Children 1st
41 Polwarth Terrace
Edinburgh EH11 1NU
helpline 0808 800 2222

Parent Network Scotland
15 Smith's Place
Edinburgh EH6 8NT
tel 0131 555 6780
A programme of information, education and support run by trained parents for parents

The Samaritans
helpline 08457 90 90 90
website www.samaritans.org.uk
Trained volunteers provide this free 24-hour telephone helpline. Callers are guaranteed absolute confidentiality.

Stepfamily Scotland
5 Coates Place
Edinburgh EH3 7AA
helpline 0131 225 5800
website www.stepfamilyscotland.org.uk
Support and information for members of stepfamilies and those who work with them.

Research, information and campaigning

Anti-bullying Campaign
185 Tower Bridge Road
London SE1 9QQ
tel 020 7378 1446
A national telephone helpline for parents whose children are the victims of bullying within the school environment. Also provides useful resources.

Children are Unbeatable!
77 Holloway Road
London N7 8JZ
tel 020 7700 0627
website www.childrenareunbeatable.org.uk
An alliance of more than 300 organisations, including professional and religious bodies, as well as many prominent individuals, which campaigns for children to have the same legal protection against being hit as adults and promotes positive, non-violent discipline.

Fathers Direct
Herald House
Lambs Passage
Bunhill Row
London EC1Y 8TQ
tel 020 7920 9491
website www.fathersdirect.com
National information service which aims to promote close relationships between men and their children.

Fostering Network
(formerly National Foster Care Association)
87 Blackfriars Road
London SE1 8HA
tel 020 7620 6400
website www.thefostering.net
An organisation committed to ensuring that all children who are fostered receive the highest standards of care. They aim to do this by assisting local authorities, agencies and individuals to work effectively in the best interests of fostered children, and by lobbying policymakers.

National Council for One Parent Families
255 Kentish Town Road
London NW5 2LX
tel 020 7428 5400
helpline 0800 018 5026
website www.oneparentfamilies.org.uk
Seeks to improve the economic, legal and social status of one-parent families.

National Family and Parenting Institute
430 Highgate Studios
53–79 Highgate Road
London NW5 1TL
tel 020 7424 3460
website www.nfpi.org
parents' website www.e-parents.org
An independent charity whose role is to bring together organisations, knowledge and know-how to enhance the value and quality of family life, to make sure that parents are supported in bringing up their children and in finding the help and information they need. Maintains the online Parent Services Directory (www.nfpi.org.uk/templates/psd), a comprehensive online database of parenting and family support services in England and Wales.

Parenting Education and Support Forum
Unit 431, Highgate Studios
53–79 Highgate Road
London NW5 1TL
tel 020 7284 8370
website www.parenting-forum.org.uk
National umbrella organisation which brings together those working in the fields of parent education and support. Aims to raise awareness of the importance of parenting and its impact on all aspects of children's development.

References

Aldgate, J. & Statham, J. (2001) *The Children Act now: messages from research*, The Stationery Office.

Brewster, A. L., Nelson, J. P., Hymel, K. P., Colby, D. R., Lucas, D. R., McCanne, T. R. & Milner, J. S. (1998) 'Victim, perpetrator, family, and incident characteristics of 32 infant maltreatment deaths in the United States Air Force', *Child Abuse and Neglect*, vol. 22, no. 2, pp. 91–101.

Brown, K. D. & Lynch, M. (1995) 'The nature and extent of child homicide and fatal abuse', *Child Abuse Review*, vol. 4, special issue, pp. 309–16.

Butt, J. & Mirza, K. (1996) *Social care and black communities: a review of recent research studies*, HMSO.

Cameron, C., Moss, P. & Owen, C. (1999) *Men in the nursery: gender and caring work*, Paul Chapman.

Cawson, P., Watam, C., Brooker, S. & Kelly, G. (2000) *Child maltreatment in the United Kingdom: a study of the prevalence of child abuse and neglect*, NSPCC.

Cleaver, H. & Freeman, P. (1995) *Parental perspectives in cases of suspected child abuse*, HMSO.

Cleaver, H., Unell, I. & Aldgate, J. (1999) *Children's needs – parenting capacity: the impact of parental mental illness, problem alcohol and drug use, and domestic violence on children's development*, The Stationery Office.

Corby, B. (2000) *Child abuse: towards a knowledge base*, 2nd edn, Open University Press.

Creighton, S. (1995) 'Fatal child abuse: how preventable is it?', *Child Abuse Review*, vol. 4, special issue, pp. 318–28.

Daniel, B., Wassell, S. & Gilligan, R. (1999) *Child development for child care and protection workers*, Jessica Kingsley.

Department for Education and Employment (1998) *Health and safety of pupils on educational visits: a good practice guide*, DfEE.

Department for Education and Employment (1999) *Sure Start for all: guidance on involving minority ethnic children and families*, DfEE.

Department for Education and Employment (2001) *National standards for under eights day care and childminding*, DfEE.

Department of Health (1995) *Child protection: messages from research*, HMSO.

Department of Health (2001a) *Children and young people on child protection registers, year ending 31 March 2001*, England, Government Statistical Service.

Department of Health (2001b) *Safeguarding children in whom illness is induced or fabricated by carers with parenting responsibilities*, Department of Health.

Department of Health, Home Office & Department for Education and Employment (1999) *Working together to safeguard children: a guide to inter-agency working to safeguard and promote the welfare of children*, The Stationery Office.

Department of Health, Department for Education and Employment & Home Office (2000) *Framework for the assessment of children in need and their families*, The Stationery Office.

Dickins, M. & Denziloe, J. (2002, forthcoming) *All together: how to create inclusive services for disabled children and their families*, 2nd edn, National Early Years Network.

Elfer, P. (1997) 'Attachment theory and day care for young children', *Highlight*, no. 155, National Children's Bureau.

Elfer, P., Goldschmied, E. & Selleck, D. (2002) *A key person in the nursery*, National Early Years Network.

Fahlberg, V. (1988) *Fitting the pieces together*, British Agencies for Adoption and Fostering.

Fahlberg, V. (1994) *A child's journey through placement*, British Agencies for Adoption and Fostering.

Farmer, E. & Owen, M. (1995) *Child protection practice – private risks and public remedies: decision-making, intervention and outcome in child protection work*, HMSO.

Finch, S. (1998) *'An eye for an eye leaves everyone blind': teaching young children to settle conflicts without violence*, National Early Years Network.

Gibbons, J. (1991) 'Children in need and their families: outcomes of referral to social services', *British Journal of Social Work*, vol. 21, pp. 217–27.

Gibbons, J., Conroy, S., & Bell, C. (1995) *Operating the child protection system: a study of child protection practices in English local authorities*, HMSO.

Goldschmied, E. & Jackson, S. (1994) *People under three: young children in day care*, Routledge.

Hague, G., Kelly, L., Malos, E., Mullender, A. with Debbonaire, T. (1996) *Children, domestic violence and refuges: a study of needs and responses*, Women's Aid Federation (England).

Health and Safety Executive (1998) *Five steps to risk assessment*, HSE.

Health and Safety Executive (1999) *A guide to risk assessment*, HSE.

Hester, M., Pearson, C. & Harwin, N. (1998) *Making an impact, children and domestic violence: training pack*, NSPCC.

Hester, M., Pearson, C. & Harwin, N. (2000) *Making an impact, children and domestic violence: a reader*, Jessica Kingsley.

Home Office (2000a) *Criminal statistics 1999*, The Stationery Office.

Home Office (2000b) *Criminal Justice and Court Services Act 2000: protection of children guidance*, The Stationery Office.

Hyder, T. & Willow, C. (1999) *It hurts you inside: children talking about smacking*, Save the Children.

Jones, D. P. H. & Ramchandani, P. (1999) *Child sexual abuse: informing practice from research*, Radcliffe Medical Press.

Kolbo, J., Blakely, E. H. & Engleman, D. (1996) 'Children who witness domestic violence: a review of empirical literature', *Journal of Interpersonal Violence*, vol. 11, no. 2, pp. 281–93.

Kosonen, M. (1996) 'Siblings as providers of support and care during middle childhood: children's perceptions', *Children and Society*, vol. 10, no. 4, pp. 267–79.

Larzelere, R. E. (2000) 'Child outcomes of nonabusive and customary physical punishment by parents: an updated literature review', *Clinical Child and Family Psychology Review*, vol. 3, no. 4, pp. 199–221.

Leach, P. (1992) *Young children under stress*, National Early Years Network.

Leach, P. (1997a) *Getting positive about discipline: a guide for today's parents*, Barnardo's & National Early Years Network.

Leach, P. (1997b) *Why speak out against smacking? Questions and answers from the physical punishment debate*, Barnardo's & National Early Years Network.

Lindon, J. (1998) *Child protection and early years work*, Hodder & Stoughton.

Lindon, J. (2000) *Too safe for their own good? Helping children learn about risk and lifeskills*, National Early Years Network.

Lloyd, E. (1996) 'The role of the centre in family support.' In C. Cannan & C. Warren (eds) *Special action with children and families: a community development approach to child and family welfare*, Routledge.

Macdonald, S. (1991) *All equal under the Act: a practical guide to the Children Act 1989 for social workers*, Race Equality Unit.

National Commission of Inquiry into the Prevention of Child Abuse (1996) *Childhood matters, Report of the National Commission of Inquiry into the Prevention of Child Abuse*, vol. 1, The Stationery Office.

NCH (2001a) *Internet safety: a parents' guide*, NCH.

NCH (2001b) *Maximising the opportunities and controlling the risks of IT for disadvantaged young people*, NCH.

Nobes, G., Smith, M., Upton, P. & Heverin, A. (1999) 'Physical punishment by mothers and fathers in British homes', *Journal of Interpersonal Violence*, vol. 14, no. 8, pp. 887–902.

NSPCC, National Deaf Children's Society, Way Ahead Disability Consultancy, Chailey Heritage (1993) *ABCD: ABuse and Children who are Disabled*, NSPCC.

Ofsted (2001) *Guidance to the national standards*, downloadable from www.ofsted. gov.uk/public/index.htm

Parton, N. (1997) *Child protection and family support: tensions, contradictions and possibilities*, Routledge.

Pilia, I. (2002, forthcoming) *Setting up a crèche: a step-by-step guide*, National Early Years Network.

Powell, J. (2001) 'Making contact', *Nursery World*, 12 April, pp. 22–3.

Public Concern at Work (2001) *Whistleblowing policy pack*, Public Concern at Work.

Reason, J (1998) *Good to work for: employing staff and working with volunteers in small groups*, National Early Years Network.

Rutter, M. (1995) 'Clinical implications of attachment concepts: retrospect and prospect', *Journal of Child Psychology and Psychiatry*, vol. 36, no. 4, pp. 459–71.

Schaffer, H. R. (1996) *Social development*, Blackwell.

Smith, T. (1996) *Family centres and bringing up young children*, HMSO.

Steinberg, L. (1993) *Adolescence*, McGraw-Hill.

Stocker, C. M. (1994) 'Children's perceptions of relationships with siblings, friends and mothers: compensatory processes and links with adjustment', *Journal of Child Psychology and Psychiatry*, vol. 15, no. 8, pp. 1447–59.

Thoburn, J., Wilding, J. & Watson, J. (2000) *Family support in cases of emotional maltreatment and neglect*, The Stationery Office.

Thompson, A. (1999) 'Doing the rights thing', *Community Care*, 11–17 March, pp. 18–19.

Webster, A. (2001) *Working with young children: divorce and separation*, Joseph Rowntree Foundation and National Early Years Network.

Wilson, G. (2001) 'Fabricated or induced illness in children: Munchausen by Proxy comes of age', *British Medical Journal*, vol. 323, 12 January, pp. 296–7.